A
THOUGHT
FOR
THE WEEK

A series of short essays in the spirit of Chassidic thought, based on the "Sidras" (weekly Torah-readings) of the week.

ADAPTED FROM THE WORKS OF

Rabbi Menachem M. Schneerson

THE LUBAVITCHER REBBE שליט"א

Vol. II

By Y. M. Kagan

Published weekly and copyright by
MERKOS L'INYONEI CHINUCH INC.
Detroit Regional Office
14000 W. Nine Mile Road
Oak Park, Michigan 48237
Tel. 398-2611

SECOND EDITION **1973**

נדפס בדפוס האחים גרויס
Printed in U.S.A. GROSS BROS. Printing Co. Inc.

PREFACE

Less than two years ago the "Thought For The Week" essays, based on talks and letters of the Lubavitcher Rebbe שליט"א , made their appearance in Detroit, Michigan, as a series of booklets disseminated weekly to the Jewish community. About two thousand copies were then being mailed weekly—a total of one hundred thousand per year. At the time of writing this preface, seventy thousand "Thoughts" are sent out every week (more than three *million* annually) to communities all over the United States, Canada and England. They are published as a weekly column in several noteworthy Anglo-Jewish newspapers in the U.S., Canada and Australia. French, Italian and Dutch translations have been undertaken by the Lubavitch offices in Paris, Milan and Amsterdam.

Hence, if growth is an attribute of *life,* then the "Thought For The Week" is certainly a vital and vibrantly 'alive' publication, fully attuned to our generation.

The "Thoughts" of the first year have already been published as a complete book, and it is with pride that we present this second volume of discourses for 5729.

I would like to express my sincere gratitude to Rabbi Nisen Mangel and Rabbi Zalman Posner for their invaluable scholarly assistance, and I hope and pray that this volume, as the first, will continue to show how the light of Chassidic teachings illuminates the path of our daily lives.

Yitschak Meyer Kagan
Oak Park, Mich.

Nissan 11th, 5729

TABLE OF CONTENTS

INTRODUCTION TO VOL. I

"A JEW MUST LIVE WITH THE TIMES"

SO STATED RABBI SCHNEUR ZALMAN, FOUNDER OF CHABAD.

THIS MEANS THAT A JEW MUST LIVE IN THE SPIRIT OF THE TEACHINGS OF THE SIDRA (WEEKLY PORTION OF THE TORAH-READING) OF THE WEEK. FROM THIS THOUGHT EMERGES A TRUE PICTURE OF THE ETERNITY OF TORAH. GONE IS THE FALSE PRESUMPTION THAT THE ANCIENT CREED GIVEN THOUSANDS OF YEARS AGO TO A TRIBE IN A DESERT, HAS NO APPLICATION TO OUR TIMES. INSTEAD, WE SEE A VITALLY RELEVANT GUIDE TO THE CONTEMPORARY JEW IN ANY SITUATION, HELPING HIM COPE WITH THE PROBLEMS OF THE TWENTIETH CENTURY.

IN THIS SPIRIT, WE PRESENT THE FIRST OF A WEEKLY SERIES OF "A THOUGHT FOR THE WEEK". THE SHORT ESSAYS IN THIS SERIES ARE MAINLY BASED ON THE FOUR VOLUMES OF "LIKUTEI SICHOS"—A COLLECTION OF TALKS BY RABBI MENACHEM M. SCHNEERSON, THE LUBAVITCHER REBBE SHLITA. WE WOULD LIKE TO EMPHASIZE HOWEVER, THAT THE TALKS IN LIKUTEI SICHOS ARE WRITTEN AT LENGTH AND WITH GREAT PROFUNDITY. SINCE "A THOUGHT FOR THE WEEK" IS INTENDED FOR THE JEWISH PUBLIC AT LARGE, AND IS RECEIVING BOTH PRESS AND RADIO COVERAGE—IT IS NOT THEREFORE A TRANSLATION, BUT AN ADAPTATION OF THE CONCEPTS IN LIKUTEI SICHOS.

FURTHERMORE, THE APPLICATION OF THESE THOUGHTS TO VARIOUS CONTEMPORARY ISSUES IS, IN MANY INSTANCES, THE WORK OF THE AUTHOR.

IT IS OUR FERVENT WISH THAT WE SHOW, THROUGH THESE DISCOURSES, HOW THE LIGHT OF CHASSIDIC PHILOSOPHY ILLUMINATES THE MANY VITAL ISSUES AND PROBLEMS OF OUR TIMES.

A THOUGHT

FOR THE WEEK

THE SIGNIFICANCE OF HUMAN ATTIRE

We are informed in this week's Sidra that when the first human beings, Adam and Eve, were created, they did not require any clothes and "were not ashamed".[1] But after their sin of eating from the Tree of Knowledge, "they knew that they were naked,"[2] and made themselves clothes to cover their bodies.

*   *   *   *

According to the opinion of many scientists, human attire is thought to have originated for two reasons: (a) as a protection against climatic conditions (heat, cold, rain, etc.) and subsequently also (b) for decorative purposes.

On closer investigation, however, it would seem that this "scientific" view is highly questionable. The cradle of the human race was in a place where climatic conditions were so temperate that clothes were not needed, yet clothes *were* worn in those early days; thus the weather theory of attire does not hold good.

According to the Torah, clothes have their origin in the change of outlook by Adam and Eve after eating from the Tree of Knowledge, as mentioned above. This radical change of outlook is explained by Maimonides.[3] His explanation as quoted in Chabad literature throws further light on the subject. Briefly it is as follows:

Man was created all good, without any evil in him. He had no evil inclinations nor did he know any temptation for physical pleasures. Consequently, all organs and parts of the body were equal to him, each one having to play its part in carrying out man's Divine mission on this earth. In his purity

I

of mind, the feeling of shame was foreign to him. For example: Just as there would be no reason for shame in teaching the Torah to someone, an act which is likened to begetting a child spiritually, in a similar way there would be no reason for shame in begetting a child physically, for here, too, man was fulfilling the Divine command of "Be fruitful and multiply".[4] In both cases, indulgence in physical pleasure was ruled out, for Adam, before he sinned, had only one consideration—the fulfillment of the Divine Will.

After the sin of eating from the Tree of Knowledge, there was born in man a consciousness of physical pleasure, of which he was not previously aware, when his spiritual self was absolutely predominant. He saw that certain parts of the body were more directly associated with the sense of physical pleasure. The exposure of those parts of the body now brought forth in him a feeling of shame on two counts: first of all, because these parts of the body were a reminder of the humiliating downfall of man into the power of lust, and secondly, because they were a source of temptation. For these reasons, man felt ashamed of his nakedness and wished to cover his body.

* * * *

The Torah is eternal. Its laws are binding in every age and under all circumstances. Hence, the Torah's laws governing modesty in attire (whose origins lie in Adam's sin, as discussed above) are relevant and applicable in all times and places, in winter and in summer, in town and at vacation resorts.

REFERENCES:
    Based on "The Significance of The Skull Cap" pp. 12-13
        [1]Genesis 2:25
        [2]Ibid. 3:7
        [3]Guide; Part I, Ch. 2
        [4]Genesis 1:28

FIRST OF ALL . . .

In this week's Sidra we are told that Noah took a pair of each species of animal into the ark, as well as *additional* Kosher animals and fowl,' so that he would be able to offer sacrifices to G-d. When he left the ark after the Flood had subsided, he carried out his intention, as the Torah states: "And Noah built an altar unto the L-rd; . . . and offered burnt offerings on the altar."[2]

* * * *

In the previous week's Sidra (Bereishis) we find a thought-provoking incident concerning 'Korbonois'—sacrifices. The Torah relates[3] how Cain and Abel both brought offerings to the L-rd. Abel, a shepherd, brought *the best* of his flock for the sacrifice, whereas Cain, a farmer, brought some mediocre fruits as an offering to G-d. The Almighty accepted Abel's offering—but rejected Cain's.

A noteworthy point in this episode is that although Cain had voluntarily brought the fruits of his toil as a gift to G-d, yet they were not accepted — for he had not brought of *the best!* Maimonides, mentioning the episode of Cain and Abel, writes:[4] "When one gives food to the needy, he should give him the best and the most delectable of his table; with the best of his wardrobe should he clothe the naked, and when he builds a house of worship he should render it more beautiful than his own dwelling, as it is written[5] '. . . all the *best* . . . is to the Almighty'."

Similarly, the best part of one's day is the very beginning, the early hours, when one is rested and refreshed, and it is *these* hours that should be dedicated to prayer and study. As soon as the Jew awakens he acknowledges G-d as his Creator, by

3

reciting 'Modeh Ani'. Afterwards, he stands in prayer before the Almighty. Subsequently he engages himself in Torah-study (even if only for a short time) and *only then*, having given of his best to G-d, does the Jew embark upon his worldly material affairs.

When the first Jewish day-schools were established in the U.S., the question arose as to which part of the day should be devoted to Torah-learning and which part to secular studies. The previous Lubavitcher Rebbe of sainted memory insisted that the children's Torah-study be reserved for the first — and best — half of the day, for " . . . all the best . . . belongs to the Almighty".[5]

* * * *

The above idea applies also to the days and years of one's life. The best years of one's life should be dedicated to the Almighty. Not, as some think, that they will postpone the study of Torah until their old age, and then begin to attend synagogue and study. The best years of one's life are the years of childhood and early youth. The yoke of adult responsibility is not yet felt; the pressure of business affairs has not yet been brought to bear, and the youth is free of the worries and burdens of family and social life. These carefree years of youth — the best years — should be utilized for studying G-d's Torah and Mitzvos.

REFERENCES:
    Based on Likuttei Sichos Vol. II pp. 326-8
        [1]Rashi on Genesis 7:2
        [2]Genesis 8:20
        [3]Ibid. 4:3-4; See also Rashi Ibid.
        [4]Hilchos Issooray Mizbeach: end, as quoted in Likuttei Sichos ibid.
        [5]Leviticus 3:16

JOURNEY OF THE SOUL

This week's Sidra opens with G-d's command to Abraham:[1] "Go out of your land and your birthplace and your father's house unto the land which I will show you." One of the ten[2] difficult tests with which G-d tested Abraham was this command — to leave his home and go to a strange land.

*   *   *   *

In the teachings of Chassidism, Abraham's journey is compared to the enforced journey and descent of the Divine soul from the spiritual realms into the physical body. Our Sages said[3] that "Each and every soul was in the presence of His Divine Majesty before coming down to this earth." This emphasizes the essential nature of the soul, its holiness and purity, and its being completely divorced from anything material and physical. The soul itself, by its very nature, is not subject to any material desires or temptations, which arise only from the physical body and "animal soul".

Nevertheless it was the Creator's will that the soul, which is "truly a 'part' of the Divine Above", should leave its "home" and its "father's house" and should journey and descend into the physical and coarse world, to be confined within, and united with, a physical body for scores of years, in a state which is absolutely repulsive to its very nature. All this is for the purpose of a Divine mission which the soul has to fulfill: to refine and elevate the physical body and its environment through a life of Torah and Mitzvos.

When the soul fulfills this mission, all the transient pain and suffering connected with the soul's descent and life on this earth are not only justified, but infinitely outweighed[4] by

5

the great reward and everlasting bliss which the soul enjoys thereafter.

From the above, one can easily appreciate the extent of the tragedy when he disregards the soul's mission on earth. For, in doing so, he condemns the soul to a term of useless suffering, not compensated for by that everlasting happiness which G-d had intended for it. Even when there are brief moments of religious activity in the study of the Torah and the practice of the Mitzvos it is sad to contemplate how often such activity is tainted by the lack of real enthusiasm and inner joy, for men donot realize that *these are the activities which justify existence.*

* * * *

If one will reflect upon the great value of Torah and Mitzvos, throught which one is enabled to attain the soul's perfection, and fulfillment of the Divine purpose, he will experience a sense of real joy at his fate and destiny, despite the many difficulties and handicaps, from within and without, which are inevitable on this earth. In this way he will be able to live up to the injunction:⁵ "Serve G-d with joy", which the Baal Shem Tov made one of the foundations of Chassidism.

REFERENCES:

Based on a letter of the Lubavitcher Rebbe שליט"א 10th of Kislev 5714
¹Genesis 12:1
²Pirkei Avos: Ch. 5:3; See also Likuttei Sichos Vol. I p. 15
³Zohar III:104b; Ibid. 29b. See also Sefer Hamaamorim 5711 p. 11
⁴Chagiga 15b; Likuttei Torah I:1d; Introduction of Ramban to Job.
⁵Psalms 100:2

KINDNESS THAT KNOWS NO BOUNDS

Each week one can find guidance and instruction for his daily life in the Sidra of that week. For the Almighty, Who is eternal, has given us a Torah which is everlasting and speaks its eternally relevant messages to every individual in every age. By studying the Torah and guiding our lives according to its teachings, we, the Jewish People, become similarly immortal and are able to withstand and survive all adversities.

* * * *

This week's Sidra describes Abraham's hospitality in these words:[1] "And he planted (or "set up") an EISHEL in Beersheba". Various interpretations are given to the word 'Eishel'. The simplest is that 'Eishel' denotes a large many-branched tree, which Abraham planted to provide protection from the hot desert sun (Beersheba is in the southern, desert portion of Canaan). Others[2] explain 'Eishel' as an orchard of fruit-trees which Abraham planted to provide refreshment for passing wayfarers.

Another opinion[3] maintains that 'Eishel' denotes an inn and that Abraham provided his guests not merely with fruit, but with food and drink and even a bed to sleep on.[4] Furthermore, Abraham went so far as to provide[5] a court of judges at the inn to settle the various disputes and questions of law that sometimes arose amongst the wayfarers — *and all this without asking for any remuneration!*

Considering that Abraham's guests were complete strangers to him, we can appreciate the greatness of Abraham's CHESSED (kindness). Abraham was not content with giving his guests "bread and water", the bare essentials of sustenance.

He deemed it necessary to provide them even with luxuries and extras — fruit, wine, all kinds of delicacies, and even a bed. As if all this were not sufficient, he felt that it was his duty to satisfy their *spiritual* needs too, and he provided a "Sanhedrin" (the aforementioned court of law) for them.

* * * *

This same extravagant kindness that Abraham displayed, is latent within every one of us! There are certain noble traits of character which we Jews have inherited from our forefathers; they have become an intrinsic part of our personality. To lend a helping hand to the needy, whether in the form of monetary charity, hospitality, or any other form of kindness, is a characteristic possessed by every Jew as a legacy[6] from Abraham and, like Abraham's trait, *it is a kindness that knows no bounds.* In the heart of every Jew is rooted the instinctive impulse to extend charity even to a complete stranger, to give him not merely the bare minimum, but extras and luxuries, and to endeavor to satisfy not only his physical wants, but also his spiritual needs.

REFERENCES:
Based on Likuttei Sichos Vol. III pp. 769-771
[1]Genesis 21:33
[2]Sotah 10a; Rashi Ibid.
[3]Ibid-R. Nechemya
[4]Midrash quoted in Bachaya on Genesis 21:33
[5]Bereishis Raba, Ch. 54:6
[6]Yevomos 79a

KINDNESS AND SINCERITY

This week's Sidra contains the account of the journey of Eliezer, Abraham's servant, to Nahor, to find a wife for Isaac. Eliezer chose Rebecca and asked her parents' consent to take her back to Canaan to become Isaac's wife. He said to them:' "And now, if you will deal *kindly* and *truly* with my master," etc.

* * * *

Eliezer's words seem rather puzzling. He was asking Rebecca's parents to show *kindness* to Abraham by letting their daughter go with him. If they would perform this act of kindness, wouldn't this in itself be the best indication that they were "dealing truly"? Why, then, did Eliezer ask them to "deal kindly *and* truly"? If one *acts* kindly and charitably towards his fellow, do not his actions *prove* the truth and sincerity of his kindness? The answer to this question is, unfortunately — "No!" There is a wide gap between "CHESSED" (kindness) and "EMESS" (truth i.e. sincerity).

This will become clearer in the light of the following freely-translated excerpts from the writings of some of the Rabbis of Lubavitch:

²*The great Rabbi Shneur Zalman of Liadi, founder of Chabad Chassidism, taught his followers to critically examine their every action and see that it be SINCERE.*

The previous Lubavitcher Rebbe of sainted memory, taught: "Some may think that true service of G-d involves world-shaking action. In reality, however, EVERY act and ANY deed is of utmost value and significance — provided it is performed with SINCERITY. For example, the simple act of

9

*uttering a 'Brocho' (blessing), but taking its meaning to heart,
the words of prayer said as they ought to be said — with genuine feeling and emotion and with the awareness that one is
standing before the Almighty; studying a verse of Chumash
(Torah) with the realization that it is the word of G-d; one
verse of T'hillim (Psalms); or the SINCERE display of love
and affection towards one's fellowman. (Of course, in order to
attain this "simple" trait of sincerity enormous effort and abun-
dant Torah-study is called for!)*

*   *   *   *

In our own era a great wall has been erected between
'CHESSED' (kindness) and 'EMMES' (sincerity). 'CHESSED'
abounds, for the Jew of today is renowned for his good-heart-
edness and generosity. But 'EMMES' is hard to find. There
are many persons who are known for their acts of 'CHESSED'.
But when it comes to 'EMMES', when they are asked to show
'CHESSED' in circumstances in which there is no opportunity
for publicity, their response is often cooler.

So wide is the gap between "Kindness" and "Truth" that
the great Torah commentator Rashi, maintains that sincere
kindness is only to be found in such acts as are exemplified by
honoring the dead! For, since the recipient will never be able
repay him, he cannot be suspected of having any ulterior mo-
tive for his kindness. Nowadays, however, even in Rashi's clas-
sic case of "Chessed Shel Emess" (sincere kindness) it is often
difficult to know whether some are present to "honor the dead"
or . . . to please the *living*.

REFERENCES:
  [1]Genesis 24:49
  [2]Hayom Yom p. 25, Adar I, 2.
       From "Eliezer's words" to " . . . Lubavitch" and from "In Our Own . . . "
       to " . . . please the *living*" is the work of the translator.

A DIGGER OF WELLS

In the course of this week's Sidra the Torah relates that Isaac dug several wells.' The first few of these wells fell into the hands of the Phillistines.' Undeterred, Isaac continued' digging, to uncover the "wells of living water."

*   *   *   *

Isaac's way of life was digging wells, removing earth and stones until fresh fountains of living water sprang up of their own accord. He did not pour water into the wells, but brought forth *their own* latent source of living water. Isaac's conduct paralleled his spiritual way of life, for in the spiritual sense he was also a "digger of wells." Throughout his life he attempted to remove the "earth and stones," the mask of materiality and corporeality of the physical world, and thereby reveal the "wells of living water," the innate spirituality of all matter.

Isaac was undismayed by the dust and dirt obstructing his path to the springs of water. He was also undeterred by the antagonism of the Phillistines and their king, Abimelech. Moreover, even when several of the precious and hard-earned wells fell into Phillistine hands, Isaac doggedly continued to dig. Logically, we might think that Isaac *should* have been discouraged by the obstacles in his path. Abimelech was, after all, the ruling monarch in that region. What is more, Isaac saw that his attempts up to that time had met with failure!

However, Isaac did not analyze the situation with cold logic. He knew that his Divine mission in life was to "dig wells" (in the spiritual, as well as the physical sense) and he committed himself to this task with a self-sacrificing devotion and with the conviction that he *would* eventually reach the source of 'living water'.

* * * *

It is relatively easy for a Jew to live in the spiritually pleasant atmosphere of Torah-study and prayer. But this is insufficient. He must also try to influence others. He should even become involved with those individuals who, on the surface, seem to be "earth and stones" — corase and lowly. It is necessary to "dig" beneath the surface until their hidden "fountains of living water", their Jewish souls, spring forth of their own accord. Also, one must be undismayed by the earth and dust that meets the eye, and undeterred by any opposition or antagonism, for Chassidic philosophy emphasizes that there *is* a Divine spark within *each and every Jew*. Hence, we are like a person who digs at a spot where he *knows* there is water, and with selfless devotion and determination will eventually reach the 'fountain of living water' — the G-dliness within each person.

REFERENCES:
    Based on Likuttei Sichos Vol. I pp. 29-31
        [1]Genesis 26:18
        [2]Ibid. v. 20-21
        [3]Ibid. v. 22

"THE LABOR OF YOUR HANDS"

This week's Sidra tells' how Jacob left the peace and security of Beersheba, where he had lived a life of Torah-study and prayer, and set out on the journey to Haran, to his deceitful uncle Laban. On the way, Jacob lay down to rest and arranged some rocks around his head to protect himself from wild beasts.

* * * *

A question arises in one's mind. If Jacob was afraid of being harmed by wild animals, why didn't he surround his *entire body* with stones? If, on the other hand, he trusted in G-d to protect him, why then did he encircle his head?

The significance of Jacob's encircling his *head* may be found in a Chassidic interpretation of the verse in T'hillim (Psalms)² "If you will eat of the labor of your hands, happy will you be, and it will be well with you." The emphasis in this verse is on the labor "of your *hands.*" Working for a livelihood, whatever form the work may take, can be in one of two ways:

The labor of one's *hands,* when one works faithfully with his hands (or any other part of his body necessarily involved in the work) yet does not submerge his entire personality in his occupation. His mind remains free, and even during business hours his thoughts often center around those matters that are close to his *inner* self.

The second way is the "labor of one's *head*", when one's mind is totally preoccupied with his business affairs. He has no time for family, for friends, or even for himself; his whole being is completely absorbed in his business.

Jacob knew that he was leaving the Yeshiva environment

13

of Beersheba, leaving a life of Torah-study and prayer, a life of holiness, a life of spirituality, and heading for a diametrically opposite kind of life. He was destined to be Laban's shepherd, to be constantly occupied with his task day and night. As Jacob himself later said:[3] " . . . by day the drought consumed me, and the frost by night; and my sleep departed from my eyes." Jacob therefore endeavored to protect his *head* — i. e. not to lose himself entirely in his occupation, but to keep his mind free to dwell on higher things, on the Torah-study and prayer that were so dear to him.

*   *   *   *

[4]Rabbi Shmuel of Lubavitch of sainted memory enjoined his followers to occupy their minds with Torah thoughts whenever they walked in the street. One businessman asked the Rebbe in amazement how such a difficult thing was humanly possible. Replied the Rebbe: "If it is possible to think business thoughts during 'Shemoneh Esray' (silent devotional prayer) . . . then it is possible to have thoughts of Torah and prayer in the street!"

REFERENCES:
   Based on Likuttei Sichos Vol. I pp. 60-63
      [1]Genesis 28:10-11
      [2]Psalms 128:2
      [3]Genesis 31:40
      [4]Sefer Hatoldos Rebbe Maharash p. 69

'YUD-TESS KISLEV'

This week we celebrate the Chassidic festival of 'Yud-Tess Kislev', commemorating the liberation from Czarist prison of Rabbi Schneur Zalman of Liadi, founder of Chabad Chassidism. Rabbi Shneur Zalman (known to Chassidim as the "Alter ('Old') Rebbe") was a disciple of the successor of the Baal Shem Tov, the founder of the Chassidic movement.

*   *   *   *

The historic day of Yud-Tess Kislev was more than a personal triumph for Rabbi Shneur Zalman. In regaining on that day his personal freedom, and the freedom to continue his teachings and work, he gained a victory for the entire Chassidic movement which had been threatened with suppression and extinction. For the Alter Rebbe was the chief exponent of the teachings of the Baal Shem Tov, who had founded the Chassidic movement about half a century earlier. It is for this reason that he was made the chief target of attack by the opponents of Chassidism, and his "Geuloh" (redemption) brought salvation to the numerous followers of the Baal Shem Tov, and to our people as a whole.

One of the great achievements of the Baal Shem Tov is that he has revealed the true nature of a Jew. While he dedicated his life to the spreading of the Torah and Mitzvos in the fullest measure, he never despaired of any Jew, no matter how much circumstances had temporarily overshadowed his Judaism. The Baal Shem Tov taught (and the Old Rebbe expounded upon it at length) that the Jew was essentially, by his very nature, incorruptible and inseparable from G-d; that "no Jew is either able or willing to detach himself from G-dliness."

It is often necessary to do no more than to "scratch the surface", and the Jew's true inner nature is revealed.

The Baal Shem Tov introduced a new brotherly relationship between Jew and Jew, based on the inner meaning of "Have we not all one Father?" By the personal example of his own dedicated work, he taught us what our attitude and approach to our fellow Jews should be. The Baal Shem Tov began his work as an assistant "Melamed" (teacher of small children), taking tender care of little children, and teaching them the Shema, Brochos, and other simple prayers. At the same time he revealed to the maturer minds of his great disciples some of the profound teachings of the "Inner Torah" — the 'Kabbala' — and the true way to serve G-d with heart and mind. This profound philosophy found its systematic expression and exposition in Chabad Chassidism.

*   *   *   *

Nowadays more than ever, it is the duty and privilege of every Jew to help educate Jewish children; "children" in the literal sense, in age, and "children" in knowledge of Judaism. As the present Lubavitcher Rebbe once said: "one's years are not to be measured by his birth certificate. A hoary elder of 70 years may, in truth, be like a baby crawling on all fours!" In a true sense, a man's education is not confined to the school-bench; it must continue throughout his life (i.e. one should try to become wiser and better every day). Thus, one must be a student and teacher at the same time, and in both cases success depends on mutual affection, on true 'Ahavas Yisroel' (love of one's fellow Jew).

REFERENCES:

Based on a letter of the Lubavitcher Rebbe שליט"א of the 12th of Kislev,

AN EMPTY ATTRACTION

In this week's Sidra, 'Vayeishev', we read[1] how Joseph became a servant in the house of Potiphar, a high officer of Pharaoh. Potiphar's wife attempted, time and time again, through devious means, to seduce Joseph. When all her efforts failed, she grasped hold of his garment, thinking that now he could not elude her. Joseph, however, slipped out of his coat, and leaving it behind in her hand, ran away.[2]

*   *   *   *

It is significant that the most 'modern' and 'progressive' circles in Judaism have not succeeded in attracting the youth. All the social attractions and intellectual 'bait' displayed by different Jewish organizations have failed to win the hearts of the younger generation and to stem the flood of their alienation from Judaism. In the episode of Potiphar's wife we may find the clue to this phenomenon.

The essence of a Jew is his *spiritual* aspect, the 'Neshama' or soul. His body is merely a vessel, a form of 'clothing' for the soul. It is the *Neshama* that is the true, inner personality of the Jew. Thus, all attempts to use material and physical attractions to capture our youth are doomed to failure. The most beautiful Jewish community centers may be built, featuring ultra-modern gymnasiums and luxurious swimming-pools; exciting dances may be arranged; dynamic speakers may be hired to speak on topics of "Jewish interest." But all these well-intended endeavors will not ultimately solve the problem of the alienated Jewish younger generation, for no matter how much we may cater to the physical tastes of our youth in order to attract them to 'Judaism', we are ultimately left, like Potiphar's wife, holding an empty garment. We have failed to communicate with their true selves; we have failed to satisfy their *true* desires.

* * * *

A patient may develop external symptoms of an internal disorder. An incompetent doctor would spend his time and energies endeavoring to cure the symptoms! Although the symptoms may temporarily be relieved by his therapy, their root cause, the internal illness, remains, and may even become worse. An experienced physician, however, will seek to diagnose the true cause of the symptoms — the disease — and by healing the disease the symptoms will automatically vanish.

This example vividly illustrates the current situation of our Jewish youth. Their unrest, their spirit of rebellion against parents, teachers, and society in general, their frantic search for *meaning* in life, their straying onto strange paths of 'hippiedom' and drug-taking, these are all symptoms of a sickness. *The sickness is the thirsting of their Neshamas for G-dliness and Torah — a thirst which cannot be quenched by artificial or bodily 'attractions', but only through drawing them, with warmth and sincere friendship, closer to a Torah-guided life.*

REFERENCES:
  Based on a free Yiddish rendition of a Discourse of the Lubavitcher Rebbe, שליט"א as it appeared in the Lubavitch News Service publication.
  [1]Genesis 39:1
  [2]Ibid. v. 7-13

THE CHANUKAH LIGHTS

Although Chanukah is celebrated for only eight days in the year, its message, and the message of the Chanukah lights are valid and compelling *all* year round.

* * * *

Two other important lights are; the lights of the seven-branched candelabrum that was lit daily in the Bais Hamikdosh (the Sanctuary in Jerusalem) and the Sabbath lights, kindled in the Jewish home every Friday evening. There are three noteworthy points of distinction between the Chanukah lights and the other two lights.

(a) The Sabbath candles must be lit *before* sunset and the lights in the Bais Hamikdosh were lit even earlier; the Chanukah lights, however, must be kindled *after* sunset, when it is already dark.

(b) The candelabrum of the Bais Hamikdosh was *inside,* in an inner sanctuary. The place of the Sabbath lights is likewise indoors on the Shabbos table. The Chanukah lights, however, are to be kindled in such a place that their light should be seen outside.

(c) Finally, the lights of the Bais Hamikdosh and of the Sabbath remain the same in number and are not increased while the number of Chanukah lights are increased every night.

* * * *

The message of Chanukah is important and timely to all Jews, but even more so to those who live in surroundings with comparatively little Jewish activity. It is precisely in such circumstances that Chanukah offers a useful lesson.

The lesson which seems to be indicated by the Chanukah Lights is that the Jew must not only light up the home (as do the Sabbath Candles), and the Synagogue and Yeshiva (substituting for the Sanctuary of old), but he has the additional responsibility of lighting up the 'outside' — his social and business environments. Moreover, when conditions are unfavorable (it is "dark" outside) it is then not enough to kindle a light and maintain it, (although this is also an achievement, for even a *little* light of Torah and Mitzvos can dispel a great deal of darkness) but it is necessary to *increase* the lights steadily, through steadily growing efforts to spread the light of Torah and Mitzvos. These ever-growing efforts contain in themselves the assurance of ever-growing success.

REFERENCES:

Based on letters of the Lubavitcher Rebbe שליט"א for Chanukah 5713 and Chanukah 5724

"JOSEPH, *MY SON*, STILL LIVES"

This week's Sidra relates¹ how Joseph revealed his true identity to his brothers and was re-united with them. It is stated in last week's Sidra that when the brothers had first come to Egypt and had met Joseph, "² . . .Joseph recognized his brothers but they did not recognize him". Why did the brothers fail to recognize Joseph? The simple explanation is that many years had elapsed since they had last seen him. They had left him an unbearded young man, and now he was a fully-bearded adult.³

*　　*　　*　　*

Chassidism offers a different interpretation of the verse " . . . ²and Joseph recognized his brothers but they did not recognize him". The sons of Jacob had all chosen to be shepherds — a quiet and peaceful occupation. Out in the fields, tending their flocks, they had little contact with the social life of the country and were undisturbed in their service of G-d, in their worship and study. The brothers of Joseph felt it necessary to select an occupation which would facilitate their leading a G-d-fearing life. They did not wish to live in an environment that would place temptations in their chosen path.

Joseph, however, was in this respect superior to them. He was able to occupy the highest administrative position in the mightiest nation of that era, and *yet* remain righteous.

The brothers did not *recognize* and could not comprehend that the viceroy of Egypt could truly remain the same G-d-fearing Joseph whom they had known, for such a way of life was above their level. In fact, not only the bothers, but even Jacob, Joseph's own father, when told that "'Joseph yet lives . . . and rules over . . . Egypt" was apprehensive lest his son, who had become the absolute ruler of the mighty Egyptian kingdom, was assimilated into Egyptian culture. It was cold comfort to Jacob that his long-lost son still lived — if he had, G-d forbid, adopted the Egyptian way of life. When his sons explained that Joseph had attained a *new and higher* level in righteousness and strength of character, Jacob experienced real joy. Only then was he truly satisfied that "Joseph, *my son,* (i.e. following *my* way of life) yet lives" — that although Joseph was viceroy of Egypt, he still conducted himself as befitted the son of Jacob.

REFERENCES:
    Based on Likuttei Sichos Vol. 1 p. 88
        [1]Genesis 45:3
        [2]Ibid. 42:8
        [3]Rashi Ibid.
        [4]Genesis 45:26
        [5]Ibid. v. 28

COMPROMISE OR COMMITMENT?

This week's Sidra opens with the words: ¹"And Jacob lived in the land of Egypt for seventeen years". According to one interpretation² of this verse, these years were the best and the most rewarding of Jacob's life, for during this period Jacob set up Yeshivos in Egypt and thereby brought a measure of refinement and holiness into the depraved life of that country; and all this he accomplished without compromising or "diluting" his own beliefs or way of life.

*   *   *   *

The Sages of the Mishna exhort: ³"Be a follower of Aaron . . . love your fellow-creatures and draw them to the Torah." The Mishna does not say 'People' but 'BRIYOS', fellow-*creatures;* implying⁴ that we should show love even towards those individuals who seemingly have no redeeming qualities whatsoever other than that they were created by the Almighty and are G-d's creatures!

Chassidim of the Alter Rebbe used to say: "Even the *sequence* and order of the Torah's laws has great significance and can teach us a great deal. The very first Mitzvah found in the Torah is G-d's command to Adam: ⁵"Be fruitful and multiply". The first precept in the Torah, and the first fundamental principle in the life of a Jew is: One Jew must try to create another, in the spiritual as well as in the physical sense; i.e. every Jew must draw and attract his fellow, with sincere affection and friendship, to come closer to the Torah, until he makes of his neighbor a better Jew, in a sense "creating" another Jew.

On the other hand, however, we must remember that the

wording of the above-mentioned Mishna is: " . . . draw them to the Torah:" We must strive to bring *them* closer to the Torah, and not, G-d forbid, to bring the Torah 'closer to them' by compromizing or diluting its laws and customs.

*　　*　　*　　*

There are some who feel that in order to draw Jews nearer to their religion, it is necessary to bring down the Torah to their level. If, for example, we will relax some of the laws governing conditions of worship in the Synagogue, many more people — they claim — would then attend the services and thereby become closer to Judaism. This argument is, however, utterly false. For the very factor that, in the first place, caused the current estrangement of some of our people from Yiddishkeit (Torah-Judaism) was the watering-down of the eternal and everlasting ideals of Torah. Hence, further compromise, rather than extinguishing the fires of assimilation, is adding fuel to its flames!

REFERENCES:
    Based on (a) Likuttei Sichos Vol. I p. 100
              (b) Ibid. p. 114
        [1]Genesis 47:28
        [2]Baal Haturim Ibid: See also Hayom Yom p. 12
        [3]Avos Ch. 1:12
        [4]Tanya Ch. 32
        [5]Genesis 1:28

THEY DID NOT CHANGE

In this week's Sidra we are told how a handful of Jews — seventy in number — managed to survive on the foreign soil of Egypt, in the midst of an overwhelmingly powerful and hostile people. They survived, not by imitating their non-Jewish neighbors and trying to hide their identity, but on the contrary, by realizing that they were different, and by guarding, most zealously and uncompromisingly, their identity and spiritual independence. Our Sages pointed out the secret of the Jews' survival in their commentary on the first verse of the Sidra: "'And these are the names of the children of Israel who came to Egypt: *'Because they did not change their names and their customs, they were redeemed from Egypt.'* " Moreover, not only did they manage to survive in spite of such adverse circumstances, but they multiplied in number and grew strong in spirit, until they received the Torah at Sinai, bringing light to the entire world and accomplishing the purpose of Creation.

*   *   *   *

This portion of the Torah, giving us the story of the first Golus (exile), contains the secret of Jewish survival in all dispersions and in all generations. This lesson should especially be remembered in our own day, when the Golus has become so tragically devastating both physically and spiritually. Jews throughout the world are surrounded by a demoralized and hostile society in which basic principles of humanity and justice are trampled upon, a world so confused that darkness is mistaken for light, and light for darkness; a world living in fear of atomic self-destruction, G-d forbid.

In this dark Golus, we Jews must take to heart more than

ever before, the teaching of our Torah which is *Toras Chayim* the Law of *Life;* that only through the preservation of our identity and spiritual independence, based on the solid foundations of our Torah and Mitzvos and nurtured through an uncompromising Torah-true education of our children, can we ensure the survival of our people, spiritually and physically, and moreover, grow and prosper.

It is only through this truly Jewish way of life that everyone individually and our people as a whole, will earn the fulfillment of G-d's blessing *Kain yirbeh v'chain yifrotz,* the blessing of growth and prosperity despite adverse circumstances, and we shall merit the true and complete Redemption through our Righteous Messiah, speedily in our time.

REFERENCES:

Based on an ecxerpt of a message yb the Lubavitcher Rebbe שליט"א dated 5717

[2]Paaneach Rozo Ibid. in name of Midrash; See also Baal Haturim Ibid.
[3]Exodus 1:12

ICY INDIFFERENCE *versus* WARM ENTHUSIASM

In every age, in any situation, the Torah, both in its legal and narrative portions, teaches us vital lessons to be applied in our daily lives. Indeed, the word 'Torah' itself comes from the Hebrew word meaning "Teaching". Even those stories that describe situations and events which could not possibly occur in our times, nevertheless contain instructive messages to all of us, for Torah is eternal.

Such is the case with regard to *all* narratives of the Torah, but much more so in the case of the stories relating to 'Yetzias Mitzrayim', the Exodus from Egypt; for there can, and should be, a spiritual 'Exodus from Egypt' in the daily religious life of every Jew'; i.e. the liberation of the Divine soul from its confinement within the Yetzer Hora (the evil inclination) — hence the command to remember the Exodus each and every day. Thus, every detail of the Torah's account of the *physical* Exodus contains directives to us regarding our own *spiritual* 'Yetzias Mitzrayim'. One such significant detail is the first plague with which the Almighty broke the proud spirit of Pharaoh and his people — the plague of blood, in which the waters of the Nile River were turned to blood.

*   *   *   *

In order to understand the significance of the plague of blood, the following introduction is necessary:

The Almighty is the ultimate source of all life². Hence, everything associated with G-dliness and holiness has vitality and life — which are characterized by WARMTH. COLDNESS, on the other hand, is the 'mark of the grave'; it is the very antithesis of life, and therefore the very opposite of holiness.

The idolatry of Egypt, the basic evil of their culture, was *coldness* — the icy indifference to G-d. This was symbolized by the *cold* waters of the Nile River which the Egyptians worshipped as a god. The very first step, therefore, towards breaking the spirit of Egypt and towards freedom from the Egyptian exile was to strike at the "waters of the river"[3] — the deathly coldness — and convert it to blood, symbolizing *warmth,* life, and vitality.

*   *   *   *

The lesson for our own spiritual 'Yetzias Mitzrayim', is that the very first undesirable trait against which we must struggle is . . . the coldness, indifference and apathy to our Judaism. It is a false notion that one can remain indifferent to G-d's Torah on the one hand, and yet refrain from actually doing evil. An icy indifference to Yiddishkeit eventually leads one to the moral corruption of Egypt. The approach to religion *should* be, one of warmth, interest and enthusiasm.

REFERENCES:
Based on Likuttei Sichos Vol. 1 p. 119
[1]Tanya Ch. 47
[2]See Avos D'Reb Nosson Ch. 34:10
[3]Zohar II:28b

THE DARKNESS BEFORE DAWN

At the close of this week's Sidra the Torah relates how the oppression and suffering of the Israelites in Egypt reached its height. So intense was the suffering of the Hebrews that Moses felt constrained to exclaim to G-d: "'Why hast Thou dealt badly towards this people ... and Thou hast not delivered Thy people." Even Moses, who was utterly devoted and faithful to G-d, could find no explanation for the extreme misery and darkness of the Exile. However, soon a most remarkable turn of events took place. *Immediately after* this *darkest* hour of the Egyptian exile, the process of the redemption was set in motion by G-d. When all hope seemed to have been lost, precisely *then* did the first rays of hope begin to shine for the Jews.

It is a well-known fact that the darkest part of the night is just before dawn. Our Sages compare exile to night. So too, when the night of the Egyptian exile seemed blackest, when the suffering of the Jews reached such a degree that even Moses complained "why hast Thou dealt badly, etc.", it was *then* that the rays of deliverance began to shine.

*　　*　　*　　*

The Talmud states[2] that while the other nations of the earth calculate the yearly cycle according to the rotation of the sun, the Jewish People bases its calendar on the rotation of the moon. For the Jews are likened to the moon, whose light wanes and diminishes, and finally seems to disappear. But it is precisely at *that* point that the new moon is born, and begins to grow steadily. Jewish history throughout the ages reflects the 'lunar cycle'. In the Egyptian exile, after reaching the lowest depths of oppression, when the long night of exile seemed at its very darkest, it was *then* that the deliverance and renewal of hope began. Such was the case in each subsequent exile.

*　　*　　*　　*

[1]There is much inspiration and encouragement to be derived from the above. There are times in one's life when it seems that the "wheel of fortune" has reached the lowest point of its cycle for him. It appears to him that his situation is beyond hope. Yet he should not lose faith and fall into despair, but should bear in mind that the darkest hour of 'Golus' (exile — both exile of our people as a whole, as well as, in a broader sense, 'exile' of each individual) comes just before the start of the 'Geuloh' (redemption).

REFERENCES:

Based on an unpublished discourse of the Lubavitcher Rebbe שליט"א as recalled by one of the listeners.

[1]Exodus 5:22-23; See also Likuttei Sichos Vol. 1 p. 120

[2]Suka 29A

Sidra Beshalach

A SCRATCH IN A SEED

This Sabbath falls between two auspicious days of the present month of Shevat. The tenth of Shevat is the Yahrzeit of the previous Lubavitcher Rebbe, Rabbi Joseph Isaac Schneersohn of sainted memory, and the fifteenth is the New Year for Trees

*   *   *   *

The Torah likens the human being to a tree[1], and the Tzadik (righteous and holy man) to a flourishing date-palm.[2] In a remarkable statement in the Talmud, our Sages declare that a Tzadik lives on forever:[3] "For just as his seed is alive, so is he alive". It is noteworthy that the word *seed* is used here rather than *descendants, children,* or *disciples.* By choosing the word *seed* in this connection, our Sages conveyed to us the specific images and ideas which this word brings to our minds. One of these ideas is the wonderful process of growth which transforms a tiny seed into a multiple reproduction of the parent, be it an ear of grain, or, in the case of a fruitseed, a fruit-bearing tree.

The education of a young child is like the planting of a seed. But it is not the easy cultivation of a simple plant. It is rather the nurturing of potential *fruit trees,* which will ultimately yield generations upon generations of their own kind. Hence, much time and effort is required to ensure that our children receive a pure and proper Torah training.

*   *   *   *

Another thought that the Talmud wished to convey to us by using the word "seed" is the care which a young plant or

31

seed requires during the growth process, and that the effect of a little extra care at an early stage is multiplied in the final product.

If a notch is carved in a mature tree, the cut does not spread and the damage is confined to the particular area where the cut was made. If, however, a scratch should be made in the *seed* prior to planting it, the entire tree could be deformed as a result of that single scratch.

Likewise, if a middle-aged man should, under trying circumstances compromize in the observance of a Mitzvah, G-d forbid, it is more than likely that the ingrained training and habit of his early years will eventually prevail and he will once again return to a full Torah observance. If, however, our *youth* is reared in a spirit of compromize, they become deprived of their natural warmth and zealous enthusiasm for a full Torah-life. This "scratch" in their soul can give rise, G-d forbid, to a spiritually crippled generation!

REFERENCES:

Based on (a) Letter of the Lubavitcher Rebbe שליט"א dated 16th of Shevat 5723

(b) Likuttei Sichos Vol. I, p. 82

¹Deuteronomy 20:19; See also Taanis 7a

²Psalms 92:13

³Taanis 5b

"NA'ASSEH VENISHMA —
FULFILL, *THEN* UNDERSTAND"

This week's Sidra tells of the giving of the Torah at Mount Sinai. G-d revealed His Will in the presence of millions of witnesses, of different outlooks, walks of life, character, etc. They, in turn, transmitted it from generation to generation *uninterruptedly,* to our day. Thus, the truth of the Torah is constantly corroborated by millions of witnesses.

Standing at the foot of the mountain in readiness to receive the Torah, the Jewish people proclaimed that they would *first* observe all its commands and *subsequently* attempt to understand them.[1] Let us examine the logic underlying this approach to Mitzvos-observance.

Man's physical body is not completely separate from his soul and it is possible to understand many things about the soul from their parallels in the body. The physical body requires a *daily* intake of certain elements in certain quantities obtainable through breathing and food consumption. No amount of thinking, speaking and studying all about these elements can substitute for the actual intake of air and food. All this knowledge will not add one iota of health to the body unless it is given its required physical sustenance; on the contrary, the denial of the actual intake of the required elements will weaken the mental forces of thought, concentration, etc. Thus it is obvious that the proper approach to ensure the health of the body is not by way of study first and practice afterward, but the reverse, to eat and drink and breathe, which in turn strengthen also the mental powers of study and concentration.

The same is true in the case of the soul. The elements which *it* requires for its sustenance are best known to its Creator and at Mount Sinai He revealed them to us, telling us that the "air" and "food" vital to our spiritual existence are ... Torah and Mitzvos.

It is told of a famous German philosopher, the author of an elaborate philosophical system, that when it was pointed out to him that his theory was inconsistent with the hard facts of reality, he replied, "so much the worse for the facts." The normal approach of a person, however, is that opinions are derived from reality and not reality from opinions. No theory, however cleverly conceived, can change the facts; if it is inconsistent with the facts it can only do harm to its adherents.

* * *

The world is a perfectly coordinated system created by G-d, in which there is nothing superfluous and nothing lacking. A man's term of life on this earth is just long enough to fulfill his purpose here; it is not a day too short nor a day too long. Hence, if he should permit a single day, or week, let alone months, to pass by without fulfilling his purpose, it is an irretrievable loss for himself and for the universal system at large. Every day that passes for a Jew without practical living according to the Torah is an irretrievable loss for himself and for all our people (inasmuch as we all form a single unity and are mutually responsible for one another) as well as for the universal order, and all theories attempting to justify such a mode of living cannot alter this fact in the least.

REFERENCES:
    Based on a letter of the Lubavitcher Rebbe א״טײ
    1) Exodus 19:8; See Tractate Shabbos 88a.

Sidra Mishpotim
MOSES WAS PUZZLED . . . !

A special portion of the Torah, "Parshas Shekalim," is read in the Synagogue this week. The portion deals with the command to every Jew to contribute half a shekel towards the building of the Mishkan—the sanctuary in the desert.

Our Sages tell' us that when Moses received the Divine command to levy a tax of a half-shekel on each adult male, he was puzzled; the half-shekel was to be an atonement for the sin of worshipping the Golden Calf. "How can the mere giving of a coin be an atonement for a sin?" thought Moses.

* * *

A question at once arises: A number of laws concerning sacrifices and offerings to be brought by the individual as atonement for his sins had already been taught by G-d to Moses. Yet Moses had never previously wondered how a mere offering could provide forgiveness for a sin. Why, then, was Moses suddenly perplexed when told of the half-shekel tax?

* * *

The Torah requires every Jew to fulfill 613 commandments. These Mitzvos are divided into two main categories — 365 Negative commandments, or prohibitions and 248 Positive precepts.

Our Sages explain² that the 613 Mitzvos parallel the 613 components of the human body. Some organs of the body have a limited, specific function — the eye to see, the ear to hear, and so on. Other organs, such as the brain and heart, not only perform a specific function, but are so vital that the entire life-force of the body is

35

vested in them.[3] Any malfunction or disease that affects *these* organs strikes at the very core of the body's vitality.

In a similar way there are, among Mitzvos, "specific" commands and "general" precepts. The first two of the Ten Commandments — "I am the L-rd your G-d" and "You shall have no other gods before Me" — are precepts that touch the very essence of the Jew's soul. Hence, a transgression against these two commandments (such as idolatry) affects the entire spiritual personality, the basic link of a Jew with his Maker.

The reason for Moses' bewilderment at the half-shekel tax can now be understood. That a particular sin could be atoned for by a sacrifice or offering did not puzzle him; but how could a half-shekel atone for *worshipping the Golden Calf* — a sin that had affected the very essence of the soul; yet the Torah terms the half-shekel ". . . an atonement for his soul?" Even if a man would give his entire wealth to G-d, would that be adequate for ransoming his *Nefesh* (soul)? Can any sum given by a person be enough of an offering for his *very soul's* redemption?

*   *   *

The answer to Moses' question lies in the special nature of the Mitzvah of the half-shekel, which will be discussed in next week's 'Thought'.

REFERENCES:
  Based on Likuttei Sichos Vol. III p. 923.
    1) Tosafos Chullin 42 a.
    2) Tikunei Zohar 30 p. 74; Tanya 23.
    3) Tanya Chapt. 9.

ONLY *HALF* A SHEKEL

The following 'Thought' is the second in the series of three on the special nature of the "Machtsis Hashekel" — the half-shekel tax that every adult male Jew was required to give towards the building of the Mishkan, the desert sanctuary.

* * *

In the Torah's command concerning the half-shekel, particular emphasis is laid on the necessity of giving *half* of a whole shekel. This is difficult to understand. Since one must always try to give the *best* to G-d,[1] why did the Torah request only *half* a shekel? Moreover, since this Mitzvah was to atone for the sin of idolatry (the sin of denying G-d's *unity*) a far more appropriate gesture of reparation would surely have been the giving of a *whole* coin, a *whole* sum; yet the Torah insists on a *half*-shekel.

To atone for the sin of the Golden Calf it was not required of the Jew that he give to the Almighty a whole shekel. Instead, he was to give *half* a shekel, signifying that the unity of G-d and His people is *not* like the union of two separate entities, in which each party remains a separate, distinct individual; rather, the oneness of a Jew with his Maker is such that together they form one whole.

The Jew without G-d is incomplete and unfulfilled, a mere 'half'; only by joining with the Almighty does he become a whole, complete person, as the Previous Lubavitcher Rebbe of Blessed Memory used to say,

37

"No Jew is either willing or able to be separate from G-dliness." As for the Almighty, the Talmud tells us that G-d says (of the Jews): "They are my children *under all circumstances;* to exchange them for another nation is unthinkable!"[2] The Jew and his Creator are two indivisible halves together forming a complete whole, a perfect unity.

* * *

Next week's discourse will bring to a conclusion the series on the half-shekel, with a discussion and explanation of the unique covenant between G-d and the Jews.

REFERENCES:
  Based on Likuttei Sichos Vol. III p. 926b.-927b.
    1) Vayikra 3:16; Ramba'm, end of Hilchos Isooray Mizbeach.
    2) Kiddushin 36a.

Sidra Tetsaveh

THE COVENANT

This week's 'thought' is the last in the series dealing with the Mitzvah of the "Mach'tsis Hashekel" — the half-shekel tax.

After Moses had pleaded with G-d to forgive the Jews for the sin of worshipping the Golden Calf, G-d gave Israel the precept of the half-shekel tax which would atone for their grievous sin (see last week's 'Thought'). Afterwards, G-d told Moses: "Behold I make a covenant..."[1]

*   *   *

The underlying concept of a 'covenant', an oath of everlasting friendship that two men swear to each other, is this: When friends are absolutely certain that their friendship is permanent, that nothing will ever affect their mutual affection — there is then no reason for them to take an oath of friendship. The friends fear, however, that time and circumstances may weaken the bond that unites them, or that some external factor may bring about a rift between them. They may therefore decide to commit themselves, through a covenant, to maintain their mutual affection — *come what may*. The obligation of the covenant is that they should always remain faithful — even if reason decrees otherwise, even if their emotions should be to the contrary.

The outcome of such a pact is, that even when one of the friends finds no rational reason for showing affection to the other, he is nevertheless bound to his comrade by the oath of friendship he took. The pact has united them as *one person* and just as one's *self*-love never ceases, so is their friendship everlasting.

This concept throws some light on a custom mentioned by the Torah[2] in connection with the making of a covenant. The parties to the pact would pass between the two halves of a slain animal. This custom is very difficult to understand. Surely a more appropriate gesture could be found for persons wishing to express their *unity* and oneness — than passing through the *disunited* halves of a whole object!

* * *

The explanation of the custom of "passing through the halves" in making a covenant, is the same as the underlying concept of the *half*-shekel, which was explained in last week's 'thought'. Each party to the covenant was to regard himself as incomplete, a mere 'half'. Hence, when G-d told Moses that He was about to make a *covenant* with the Jews, He was emphasizing once again the lesson of the half-shekel — that a Jew and his Creator are two indivisible halves, together forming one whole, a perfect unity.

REFERENCES:
  Based on Likuttei Sichos Vol. III p. 928b.-929 and on Likuttei Torah :Nitsovim.
    1) Exodus 34:10.
    2) Genesis 15:9-11 ; Jeremiah 34:18.

Sidra Ki Sisso

PURIM ... AND ASSIMILATION

One of the Mitzvos connected with the festival of
Purim, which we have just celebrated, is "Shallach
Monos"—sending of two kinds of foods to a friend.
One explanation of this Mitzvah is that by observing
it we rectify a transgression committed by some of our
people in the days of the Purim story. As related in
the Megillah, Achashveirosh (King of Persia) arranged a sumptuous banquet. The food and drinks
served at this feast were not kosher. At this same feast
the holy vessels of the Beis Hamikdosh (Sanctuary in
Jerusalem) which were in the custody of the Persian
conquerors, were desecrated. Nevertheless, some Jews
participated in the banquet and partook of the trefah
food. Purim, of course, commemorates the downfall of
Haman after the Jews had completely returned to G-d.
The celebration includes sending "Shallach Monos",
food and drink, demonstrating our loyalty to G-d, and
particularly to His laws of Kashrus.

There is another, more profound explanation of
this precept.

Persia, in those days, was the mightiest empire in
the world. It boasted the most advanced civilization
of the time. On the other hand, the Jewish people at
that time were in despair. The Holy Land and the Beis
Hamikdosh lay in ruins. It seemed to some that G-d
had abandoned His people. There were even calculations, based on the writings of the Prophets, that the
exile should end, yet the promised liberation had not
come. The Midrash comments that this, in fact, was

41

one of the reasons why Achashveirosh made that pomp-
ous feast and dared to profane the holy vessels.

Under those circumstances, when the head of this
mighty empire arranged the royal feast, inviting to it
representatives of all nations, including the Jews, many
Jews could not resist the temptation. They were not
deterred by the fact that this banquet was to mark the
beginning of a "new era" of complete assimilation;
they were deluded by the beckoning slogan of "no com-
pulsion". Thus, Jews actually became a party to the
profanation of the holy vessels.

Symbolically, the profanation of the holy vessels of
the Beis Hamikdosh marked the desecration of the
Divine soul, the "sanctuary" of every Jewish man and
woman. The purpose of this Divine spark is to illuminate the environment with the light of the highest Divine ideals. Far from fulfilling their soul's mission upon
this earth, those weak Jews encouraged assimilation and
darkness. By partaking of the "food" of Achashveirosh
they contaminated both their bodies and souls.

*   *   *

Purim reminds us not to be carried away by the
outer sparkle of alien civilizations and cultures, and to
resist assimilation despite all its blandishments.

REFERENCES:
Based on a Purim letter of the Lubavitcher Rebbe שליט"א

SELF-SACRIFICE — THEN AND NOW

The central theme of Purim — the festival which highlights the current month of Adar — is the miraculous deliverance of the Jews from the decree of annihilation of the entire Jewish people, "young and old, infants and women, in one day."[1] The Midrash relates how the decree was nullified:

"After Haman had built the gallows, on which to hang Mordechai, he went to Mordechai and found him sitting in the Beis Hamedrash (study-hall) surrounded by small children dressed in sackcloth, studying the Torah, and weeping. Haman counted them and found twenty-two thousand children. He cast upon them iron chains and ordered watchmen to stand guard over them and said: 'tomorrow I will kill these children and afterwards I will hang Mordechai.' The mothers of the children brought them bread and water and said to them: 'Our children, eat and drink before you go tomorrow to your death, and do not die while fasting.' The children immediately laid their hands on the holy books that they were studying and swore: '... by the life of Mordechai our teacher, we will neither eat nor drink; fasting we will die!' They all burst into heartrending sobbing until their cries ascended to heaven. The Almighty heard their cries and His pity was aroused; He rose from the Throne of Judgement and sat upon the Throne of Mercy."[2]

The Mishna states: "He who reads the Megilla 'backwards' does not fulfill his duty."[3] The Baal Shem Tov declared that "reading backwards" also implies

43

thinking that the miracle of Purim was valid only 'back in those days,' but not now.

Thus we are forcefully reminded that all the events that took place on Purim apply equally today. Although no such decree, G-d forbid, now hangs over our people (on the contrary, Jews can, thank G-d, live in peace and prosperity) the secret of Jewish survival remains the same: proper education of Jewish boys and girls to the degree of *Mesiras Nefesh* (self-sacrifice) for Yiddishkeit.

This is precisely the basic function of Jewish teachers and parents; to gather Jewish children (children in the literal sense of the word, as well as "children" in terms of knowledge of G-d's Torah and Mitzvos) and imbue them with the feeling that they are "children of G-d, your G-d,"[4] and that they should continue to forge the golden chain of their ancestral tradition to the point of veritable self-sacrifice for the preservation of the Jewish way of life, the way of the Torah and Mitzvos.

REFERENCES:
 Based on a letter of the Lubavitcher Rebbe שליט״א   dated 7th Adar 5728, to the opening of a new Lubavitch community center in London, England.
    1) Esther 3:13.
    2) Midrash Rabah Esther, 9:5.
    3) Megillah 17a.
    4) Deuteronomy 14:1.

TO THE JEWISH WOMAN

These days join the festivals of Purim and Pesach. It is an appropriate time for some reflection on the important historical role Jewish women played in these festivals and on the lessons we may learn from their contribution.

* * *

Because of the time-consuming duties of housekeeping, bringing up children, etc., that are woman's primary responsibilities, the Torah frees her from the obligation of performing many of the Mitzvos. However, she is required to participate in the special Mitzvos connected with the festivals of Purim and Pesach, such as hearing the reading of the Megillah and reading the Haggada. Our Sages explain that these Mitzvos are given to women because of their share in bringing about the great deliverances commemorated by Purim and Pesach.[1]

The Megillah tells us of the crucial part which Esther had in the miracle of Purim. It was Esther who took the first step towards bringing the redemption, by telling Mordechai, "Go and gather all the Jews who are in Shushan and fast for me. Do not eat or drink for three days, night and day; I and my maidens will also fast."[2] After the three days of fasting and praying, Esther came before the King in the throne-room to intercede for her people. In coming before the king without being summoned she risked her very life, for anyone entering the throne-room uninvited was subject to the penalty of death. It is not surprising therefore, that Esther's vital role is recognized by having both the

Book of Esther and the Fast of Esther named for her.

As for Passover, our Sages emphasize in the Midrash that it was the Jewish women who kept up the courage and spirits of the men in those most trying times of Egyptian bondage. Moreover, they raised the generation worthy of receiving the Torah at Sinai and who later entered the Promised Land, the everlasting inheritance of our people.

The part played by Jewish women on these two occasions was somewhat different. In the case of Passover, the woman's influence was concentrated in the home and family, displaying all the true feminine Jewish virtues of modesty, piety and faith. In the case of Purim Esther showed that where Divine Providence places a Jewish woman in a position of social prominence and influence, she uses it wholly for the benefit of her people and is ready to sacrifice her very life for them.

* * *

Jewish Women, Mothers and Daughters! Follow the example of your mothers of old and keep alive the great tradition of Jewish womanhood. Remember, the future of our people is your responsibility!

Your sincere devotion to your responsibilities will surely bring you G-d's help. Not only will all difficulties and obstacles disappear—as in the case of Esther— but you will receive generous Divine blessings for the fulfillment of all your needs and those of your family, materially and spiritually.

REFERENCES:
   Based on a letter of the Lubavitcher Rebbe שליט"א   dated 12th of Adar II, 5714.
      1) Shulchan Aruch 689 (see commentaries and sources).
      2) Esther 4:16.

THE FIFTH SON (Part i)

The festival of Pesach is dominated by the central theme, "When your son asks you."[1] Indeed the entire Passover "Haggadah" (a book read at the Seder service, recounting the story of the Exodus from Egypt) is based on the Torah's command, "You shall tell your son" — the word *Haggadah* itself meaning "telling" or "narrative."

* * *

During the Seder service we read in the Haggadah that ". . . the Torah speaks of four sons, one wise, one wicked, one simple, and one who does not even know how to ask a question." The Haggadah then proceeds to tell us the questions posed by each of these 'sons,' and the reply which we are to give to each of them.

The Wise Son inquires about the special Mitzvos of Passover and we are to tell him in detail all the laws and customs of the festival. The Wicked Son asks: "What is this service to you?" By saying "to *you*" he excludes himself from the Jewish community, and we are told to reply to him sharply. The Simple Son asks: "What is this all about?" In reply we are to tell him of the Exodus from Egypt. As for the son who does not know how to ask, it is for us to open the conversation with him, as the Torah says, "You shall tell your son on that day, saying, 'This is on account of what the L-rd did for me when I went forth from Egypt'."[2]

* * *

While the Four Sons differ from one another in their reaction to the Seder, they have one thing in common: they are *all* present at the Seder. Even the "Wicked" son is there, taking an active, though rebellious, interest in what is going on in Jewish life around him. This, at least, justifies the hope that some day also the "Wicked" one will become wise, and all Jewish children attending the Seder will become conscientious, observant Jews.

Unfortunately, in our time of confusion and spiritual bankruptcy, there is another kind of a Jewish child — a "fifth son," who is conspicuous by his absence from the Seder; the one who has no interest whatsoever in Torah and Mitzvos, laws and customs, who is not even aware of the *Seder-shel-Pesach,* of the Exodus from Egypt and the subsequent Revelation at Sinai.

This presents a grave challenge, which should command our attention long before Passover and the Seder-night, for no Jewish child should be forsaken. It is one of the vital tasks of our time to exert all possible effort to awaken in the young generation (as also in those who are advanced in years but still immature in deeper understanding) a fuller appreciation of the values of Torah Yiddishkeit, a full and genuine Yiddishkeit, instead of misrepresented, compromised, diluted "Judaism," whatever its label or trade-mark. Together with this appreciation will come the realization that only true Yiddishkeit can guarantee the existence of the individual, of every Jew, at any time, in any place, and under any circumstances.

REFERENCES:
  Based on a letter of the Lubavitcher Rebbe אשליט״א dated Passover 5717.
    1) Exodus 13:14.
    2) Exodus 13:8.

THE FIFTH SON (Part ii)

Last week we discussed the "four sons" of the Passover Seder. It was mentioned that there is, unfortunately, another kind of Jewish child who is conspicuous by his absence from the Seder. A challenging and pertinent question is: What brought about this regretably-all-too-common phenomenon of the "fifth son"?

* * *

The 'Fifth Son' is the result of an erroneous psychology and misguided policy on the part of some immigrants arriving in a new and strange environment. Finding themselves a small minority, and encountering social and economic difficulties, some parents had the mistaken notion, which they transmitted to their children, that the way to overcome these difficulties is to become quickly assimilated into the new environment by discarding the heritage of their forefathers and abandoning the Jewish way of life. Finding that this process leads to the discomfort of inner spiritual conflict, some parents resolved to spare their children this conflict *altogether*. They simply gave their children *no* Jewish education or training.

To justify the desertion of their religion and appease their stricken conscience, it was necessary for them to devise some rationale. They persuaded themselves, and in turn their children, that the Jewish way of life, with the observance of the Torah and Mitzvos, was incompatible with their new surroundings. They sought, and therefore also "found," faults with the true Jewish way of life; while in the non-Jewish environment everything seemed to them only good and attractive.

By this attitude these parents hoped to assure their children's existence and survival in the new environment. But what kind of existence is it, if everything spiritual and holy is traded for the material? What kind of survival is it, if it means the sacrifice of the soul for the amenities of the body?

The tragic consequence of this utterly false approach was, that thousands upon thousands of Jews have been severed from their fountain of life, from their true faith, and from their fellow Jews. Deprived of spiritual life, there has risen a generation of children who no longer belong to the "Four Sons" of the Haggadah, not even to the category of the "Wicked" one. They are almost a total loss to their fellow Jews and to true Yiddishkeit.

* * *

The Exodus from Egypt and the Festival of Pesach are forceful reminders that an attempt to emulate the environment does not lead to survival, deliverance and freedom. These come from staunch loyalty to our traditions and the Torah way of life. Our ancestors in Egypt were a small minority, and lived in the most difficult circumstances. Yet they preserved their identity, and with pride and dignity, tenaciously clung to their own way of life, traditions and uniqueness. Precisely in *this* way was their existence assured, and eventually their deliverance from every slavery, physical and spiritual.

REFERENCES:
Based on a letter of the Lubavitcher Rebbe א״שליט   dated Passover 5717.

REMEMBER ... AND RELIVE

We have just celebrated the festival of Passover, when we recall that great event at the dawn of our history, the liberation from Egyptian slavery of our people in order to receive the Torah as free men.

*   *   *

Memory and imagination enable one to associate with an event in the past, and in so doing to relive or re-experience those feelings and emotions which were felt at the time of the event. For only physically is the human being limited by time and space; for the mind there are no such barriers. The greater the supremacy of the spiritual over the material, the more easily can one associate with a past event and more fully experience its message and inspiration.

Our Sages comment on the verse: "And these days shall be *remembered* and *done*"[1] that as soon as those days are *remembered,* the same Divine influences that brought about those miraculous events of old, are stirred again by the process of recollection and remembrance.[2] The singular atmosphere that surrounded the original events of the festival, with all its soul-stirring aspects, becomes re-awakened and actually 're-occurs' as we remember the event each year with the advent of the festival.

This is one of the reasons why we are to *remember* the liberation from Egypt in every generation, every day. In fact, every Jew must view himself, every day, as though he personally had been liberated on that day from Egypt.[3] Every day the Jew must practice, and seek to experience, an exodus and liberation from the "Egypt" within him — the material and physical distractions, the obstacles and limitations imposed upon his spirit by his body and its desires.

So we see that the spiritual counterpart of the historic event of the Liberation from Egypt is the release of the Divine Soul from its corporeal imprisonment. This must be experienced every day, constantly, in order to enjoy true freedom, for the worst and most painful type of bondage is the slavery of the individual to his own desires and passions.

When the Jew achieves such inner freedom — an accomplishment possible only through living by Torah and its precepts — he experiences a feeling of complete inner harmony, contentment and peace of mind, which is the prelude to freedom and peace in the world around him, to be ushered in with the coming of our righteous Messiah.

REFERENCES:
    Based on a letter of the Lubavitcher Rebbe   א״טיש   dated Nissan 5713.
      1) Esther 9 :28.
      2) Rama'z in Tikkun Shovovim, quoted in Lev David Chap. 29.
      3) Haggadah ; Tanya Chapt. 47.

ON THE SIGNIFICANCE OF 'SEFIRAH'

These days between the festivals of Passover and Shovuos are marked by the custom of 'Sefirah' — counting the days of the "Omer." We begin counting immediately after the day of the liberation from Egypt, and we count for forty-nine days, at the end of which we celebrate Shovuos — the festival of Receiving the Torah, marking the climax of the liberation.

* * *

There is a famous teaching of the Baal Shem Tov, the founder of Chassidism: "A Jew should always attempt to find, in everything he sees or hears, a lesson and guide towards better service of the Almighty." This is true of *"everything* one sees or hears," and is certainly so with regard to the festivals of our Torah, which contain important instructions for us in our daily lives. Let us examine one such vital lesson that is taught by the Festival of Pesach and the observance of 'Sefirah':

For centuries the children of Israel were enslaved in Egypt, in a bondage of body and spirit and were in great danger of assimilation. In fact, they had descended to such a low spiritual level that when Moses brought them the message of their deliverance from Egyptian bondage, they did not listen to him, "because of lack of spirit and hard labor."[1]

However, after their liberation from enslavement, they attained, in a comparatively short time, the highest spiritual level man can reach. Every man, woman and child of Israel was fit for Divine Revelation at Mount

Sinai, worthy to receive the highest knowledge and inexhaustible source of wisdom and faith for all generations to come.

This shows that every person is capable of rising from the lowest depths to the loftiest spiritual heights in a remarkably short time, if only he has the sincere and wholehearted desire and will to do so.

The children of Israel had such desire and will. When they learned of the real purpose of their liberation — the receiving of the Torah at Mount Sinai, they were impatient for that moment and counted every day in eager anticipation of the event.[2] For this reason we too count the days of Sefirah, re-creating the feelings of our fathers in our own hearts.

* * *

The aforesaid has an additional encouraging message for everyone: When a person displays a resolute will to rise above his level, G-d helps him to achieve his goal by freeing him from all handicaps which stand in his way, so that *every* Jew *can* fulfill his soul's mission on this earth.

REFERENCES:
   Based on a letter of the Lubavitcher Rebbe שליט"א
    1) Exodus 6:9.
    2) Shivlay Haleket, Aroogah 8 (Seder Atzeress 236) ; Ra'n, end of Pesachim.

Sidra Acharei-Kedoshim

ELASTIC TIME

The current period of 'Sefirah' connects the festivals of Pesach and Shovuos. We begin counting the days of the Omer immediately after the day of the Exodus from Egypt, the day of liberation from slavery, and continue for forty-nine days, when we celebrate the festival of Receiving the Torah, marking the climax of the liberation.

*   *   *

The purpose of counting or measuring is to ascertain the exact number or measure of a certain thing, the quantity of which is variable. A population census, for example, is taken from time to time, since the population can either increase or decrease. Similarly, statistics are kept of various fluctuating phenomena. Were these phenomena stationary and unchangeable, or were they uncontrollable, there would be no real purpose served in reviewing such statistics periodically.

Time is an element over which man has no control or influence. Time moves inexorably. We can neither slow its march, nor accelerate it, nor can we change its dimensions and make an hour last more or less than sixty minutes. What then is the purpose of Sefirah? However, although Time is unchangeable and beyond our control, this is only partially true. Actually, Time possesses, for each individual, vast potential for achievement. In fact, while man's influence over things under his direct control is limited, his influence over Time is, in a sense, unlimited. For Time is like a 'vessel' which is highly elastic, with an infinite absorptive capacity. It has the power of expanding or contracting, depending upon how much or how little is put into this 'vessel.' We can fill our time with unlimited content, or squander it completely. The very same unit of Time may be an eternity to one person, or shrink to nothingness for another. *The true measure of time is not its quantity but what was achieved during that period.*

*   *   *

It is true that we cannot alter the passage of time, either stretching it or contracting it, yet Sefirah teaches us that each unit of time, not necessarily a long period, but even a day, offers us limitless possibilities. Although human life is limited to a certain number of years, the use to which these years are put, and what may be accomplished in them, is unlimited.

REFERENCES:
Based on a letter of the Lubavitcher Rebbe שליט״א

"SIX DAYS SHALL WORK BE DONE"

This week's Sidra, Emor, contains the following command pertaining to the Shabbos (Sabbath): "Six days shall work be done; but the seventh day is a Sabbath of rest . . . you shall do no manner of work."[1]

* * *

How meaningful are even the most simply worded of G-d's commands! In fact, there is significance even in the sequence and order of the Torah's words concerning the Shabbos day. First the Torah commands us to work for six days and *then* we are commanded to rest on the seventh.

The calendar week begins on Sunday. Prevalent custom has designated this first day as a day of rest, with the working week following. The Torah, however, sets the working week first, to be *followed* by the day of rest, the holy Shabbos. "Six days shall work be done . . ." and only *then* ". . . the seventh day is a Sabbath of solemn rest,"[1] etc. — the exact reverse of general practice. This precedence of labor before rest indicates that the purpose of man on earth is not to while away his time indolently, but to *work* for his spiritual as well as his own material welfare and for that of his community.

* * *

Immediately following the creation of Adam, the Torah states: "And the L-rd G-d took Adam, and placed him in the Garden of Eden to work it and guard it."[2] The meaning of this verse is as follows: it was G-d's Will that man work to develop within himself the spiritual qualities with which he had been endowed by G-d. In this way man could become an active "partner" of G-d in the development and revelation of his own and the world's innate good qualities. Having informed us that our purpose in the world is to "...work it and guard it,"[2] G-d gave us the Torah (derived from the Hebrew word hora'a — "teaching") to teach us how we are to 'work' and 'guard' the world. With the Torah as our guide we are able to fulfill our task and bring fulfillment to ourselves and to the world around us.

REFERENCES:
  Based on a letter of the Lubavitcher Rebbe שליט״א printed in "From Day to Day"—a Jewish calendar for the young scholar.
     1) Leviticus 23:3.
     2) Genesis 2:15.

Sidra Behar-Bechukosay

A LETTER ON SHABBOS OBSERVANCE

In conjunction with last week's "Thought" about the significance of the Shabbos, we bring here an adaptation of a letter concerning Sabbath observance, written to an individual by the Lubavitcher Rebbe שליט״א

Dear Mr. _____,

I have received your letter in which you inform me about yourself and your family and present before me your problem: You operate a hardware store, which is the source of your weekly income and as Shabbos is the busiest day in the week, you have kept your store open on Shabbos, but the violation of the Shabbos bothers you, and you ask my advice.

I want to tell you first of all that I was very pleased to hear that the desecration of the Shabbos disturbs you to the depth of your heart. It shows that your Jewish heart is alive and active and strongly objects to your doing something wrong — wrong not only for your soul, but also for your body, for with the Jew the body and soul are closely united to form one whole, and there can be no thing which is hurtful to the soul and yet not be hurtful to the body.

Before answering your question, I want to make the following observations by way of introduction:

Jews, in general, and faithful ones in particular, have no doubt that G-d created the world and guides it. Nor is there any doubt that the Ten Commandments are from G-d, and among them the fourth: "Remember the Shabbos day to keep it holy . . . you shall do no work on it."

It is equally certain that G-d, Who created man, also provides him with opportunities to sustain himself. It would be illogical to imagine that G-d would compel anyone to obtain his livelihood in a manner contrary to His will, and particularly, contrary to His will expressed in the Fourth Commandment of keeping the Shabbos day holy.

One more point I wish to underscore. The money one earns is not an end in itself; it is but a means to obtain one's needs. Obviously, rather than first earning money and then, G-d forbid, spending it on medical care, it is preferable to forego both the earnings and the medical expenses—and be well. The important thing, therefore, is not the money earned, but the assurance that the money would be well spent and properly enjoyed.

After this preface, let us consider your case.

You have the privilege of being born a Jew, which means that you have been given the possibility to go through life along the Jewish path, the path of Torah and Mitzvos, of which Shabbos observance, Kashrus, Taharas Hamishpocha (family purity through Mikvah), and the like, are fundamentals.

There can be no doubt that if you determine to follow the path of Torah and Mitzvos, the Almighty will provide you with a kosher means of livelihood. This does not mean, of course, that the path will be easy from the outset. For reasons often beyond our comprehension, G-d may make the path difficult with trials and tests, while an easier road presents itself easier and better, that is, in the mind of the one who is put to the test, but a road which involves the neglect of a Mitzvah or a transgression of a prohibition (Averah). Such a test may be a severe one, for example, when it appears that so many Jews who unfortunately desecrate the Shabbos seem to prosper, perhaps more than those who struggle to observe it.

It is certain, however, that it is not so. The ultimate happiness of a Jewish man or woman can only be found through Torah and Mitzvos. In your case it depends on your observing the Shabbos.

Consequently, as a friend of yours and in compliance with the Mitzvah of 'Veohavto l'reacho komocho' (love your fellow as yourself) which is also a fundamental of Torah, it is my duty to advise you to base your life in general, and means of livelihood in particular, upon the commandments of our Torah. Do not be influenced in any way by the difficulties that may arise in the beginning, even loss of earnings. Be absolutely firm in your faith that the Almighty will eventually provide for all your needs in a kosher way, and you and your wife and children will lead a happy Jewish life, a life of complete harmony between the physical and spiritual, between the material needs and the Divine soul. For, to quote a saying by my saintly father-in-law of blessed memory: A Jew neither desires, nor can he be separated from G-d.

I am looking forward to hearing good news from you, and conclude wishing you success in arranging your affairs materially and spiritually.

Cordially,

Rabbi Menachem M. Schneerson

TORAH—THE SECRET OF OUR EXISTENCE

Shovuos, the festival of Receiving the Torah, is almost with us. It is an appropriate time to consider the question: What is the secret of our existence? What has helped our people survive from that moment when we were declared to be a "kingdom of priests and a holy nation," right up until the present day?

Was it wealth or strength?

An objective survey of the long history of our people will show that it was not material wealth nor physical strength that helped the Jewish people to survive through the ages. Even during the most prosperous times under the united monarchy of King Solomon, the Jewish people and state were insignificant by comparison with such contemporary empires as Egypt, Assyria and Babylonia.

Was it a homeland?

That it was not statehood or homeland is clear from the fact that most of the time, by far, our people possessed no independent state and has lived in the diaspora.

Was it a common language?

That it was not the language, is likewise clear from the fact that even in Biblical times Aramaic began to supplant the Holy Tongue as the spoken language. Parts of the Scripture and almost all of our Babylonian Talmud, the Zohar, and much else, are written in that language. In the days of Saadia and Maimonides, Arabic was the spoken language of most Jews, while later Yiddish and other languages predominated.

Was it a common culture?

Nor was it any common *secular* culture that preserved our people, since that changed radically from one era to another.

The only common factor throughout the ages of Jewish history in all lands, and under all circumstances, is the Torah and Mitzvos which Jews have observed tenaciously in their daily lives.

To be sure, there occasionally arose dissident groups that attempted to break away from Torah Judaism, such as the idolatry movements during the first Beth Hamikdosh, the Hellenists during the second, Alexandrian assimilationists, Karaites, etc., but they did not survive and have all but disappeared. Considered without prejudice, our adherence to the Torah and the practice of its mitzvos in our every-day life must be recognized as the essential factor of our existence and survival.

The secret of our existence is in our being "a people that dwell alone,"[1] every one of us, man or woman, believing in the One G-d, leading a life according to the one Torah, which is eternal and unchanging. Our 'otherness' and independence of thought and conduct are not our weakness but our strength. Only in this way can we fulfill our function imposed on us by the Creator, to be unto G-d a "kingdom of priests and a holy nation,"[2] thereby being also a "... 'treasure' for all humanity."[3]

REFERENCES:
    Based on a pastoral letter of the Lubavitcher Rebbe שליט"א for Rosh Hashana 5718.
        1) Numbers 23:9.
        2) Exodus 19:6.
        3) Ibid 5.

SHOVUOS AND TORAH

The current Yom-Tov (festival) of Shovuos, commemorates the Receiving of the Torah — G-d's greatest gift to the Jewish nation.

* * *

Just as G-d Himself is infinite and unlimited, so is the Torah (being G-d given) infinite. Every individual may view Torah in a different light. Some regard Torah as a means to gain reward and avoid punishment, as promised in the Torah. To others, the Torah is a guide to good, wholesome living, and an ideal social system. Both of these views, however, are limited.

Chassidic teachings go much deeper than these views of Torah; Chassidism delves into the profound inner significance of the Torah. According to the explanation of Chabad Chassidic philosophy, the underlying purpose of the Torah is to serve as the link between the Creator and creation.

A brief explanation of this point is called for:

Creation is generally divided into four "kingdoms": The first and lowest is the realm of *inanimate* inorganic matter such as rock, earth or water. Next is the level of *plant* life, above which is the *animal* kingdom. Finally, on the highest scale of creation is the thinking, speaking, *human being*. All creation is finite — but the Creator (G-d) is infinite. There is no common denominator between the two. In respect to the Creator there is no difference among the "Four Kingdoms" of creation; there is no difference (in respect to the Almighty) be-

63

tween the highest intellect among men, and the crudest stone! Both are creations, and as such have no co-relationship with the Creator. That is why it is impossible for even the most brilliant human being to grasp G-d with his intellect.

However, G-d gave man a possibility to approach and commune with Him. G-d showed us how an insignificant creature can reach beyond his inherent limitations and commune with G-d the Infinite, through studying His Torah and obeying His commandments.

* * *

Here lies the most important aspect of the Torah and Mitzvos. They provide the means for us to rise above our status as creatures, mortals. We are capable now of attaining a far higher degree of perfection than we ever could with our own created, limited, gifts of mind.

REFERENCES:
    Based on a letter of the Lubavitcher Rebbe שליט"א

Sidra Nosso

SANCTUARY IN THE DESERT

The following is an adaptation of a letter sent by the Lubavitcher Rebbe שליט״א to the annual convention of "N'Shei Chabad", Lubavitch Women's organization.

I send my greeting and blessing to the participants and members of the Agudos N'shei uBnos Chabad, on the occasion of your Annual Convention. May G-d help you put into effect all the vital plans that will be adopted at the Convention, and translate them into ever growing accomplishments, for the ultimate purpose of "thought" and "speech" is deed.

The founder of Chabad, under whose banner you carry on your good work, said: "It is necessary to live with the times." This means that it is necessary to live according to the instructions and teachings contained in the Sidra of the week. I hope that the Convention will bring new life and vitality (from the source of life—our Torah) into your work—especially into those phases of your work which are noted in the Sidras of this week.

Your convention is taking place during the week between the Sidras of Bamidbor and Nosso. A subject common to both is the Sanctuary in the desert and the distribution of the duties connected with it when it was carried from place to place. Even when Jews find themselves in a wilderness, they have the ability to erect a Sanctuary for the Divine Presence to dwell among them, and within each of them.

There is a physical desert, a place of desolation, of harsh climate, of poisonous snakes. There is a spiritual desert too, that may be found even in a flourishing garden. Torah teaches us that when Jews find themselves in such a spiritual desert, it is possible, in fact imperative, to erect a Sanctuary, carry it as we go forward, until eventually the environment turns from a desert of the spirit into the blessed and holy

65

land, with the fulfillment of the true and complete Redemption, through our Righteous Moshiach.

Here is guidance for all Jews, especially for Jewish women, for, the Torah tells us, the Jewish women responded before the men when the Sanctuary was to be erected in the desert. In the spiritual desert, in which some of our people find themselves, the desolation and aridity in Yiddishkeit in general, not to mention in the Chassidic way of life, you have a challenge— and also a great and eternal privilege. You can be among the first to bring about a radical change in the prevailing conditions through extending the influence of full and maximal Yiddishkeit. This will turn the environment into a Sanctuary, a fitting place for the Divine Presence. I hope that you will fulfill this, your life duty, with devotion and alacrity.

I especially wish to call attention to the necessity of including in your sphere of activity not only the adults and youth, but also very young children. Experience has clearly shown that when we bring up a child in a certain manner from the earliest age, we can be assured of greater success and of greater and better fruits.

COUNTING ... AND CONTENT

We are now reading the Sidros of the Book of Bamidbar. The very first Mitzva mentioned in Bamidbar is: "Take the number of all the congregation of the children of Israel."[1] The book is called "Numbers"[2] because it opens with the command to take a census of the Jews.

* * *

In the process of counting, the *content* of the numbered persons or things is entirely irrelevant. A census of the population reveals nothing about the quality of the people; mere counting takes no account of the greatness or smallness of the person. The greatness of the numbered individual makes no difference; the greatest is counted as no more, and the smallest as not less, than one.

Apparently, we are told nothing about the quality of the Jewish people merely by knowing how many they numbered. This leads to a challenging question. If counting is so superficial that it does not reflect the content or importance of the numbered, why is it the first and basic mitzva of this book of the Torah, to the extent that the entire volume of Bamidbar is called "The Book of Numbers?"

* * *

Within the complex of the regulations of Kashrus there is a principle known as "Bittul" or nullification. Under certain conditions a piece of "treyfa" (nonkosher) food can become "nullified" and lose its nonkosher status. For example, if a small piece of treyfa meat becomes intermixed with a few pieces of kosher meat so that it is impossible to recognize which is the treyfa piece, then under certain circumstances it may be permissible to eat *all* the meat. The treyfa piece is considered to have become "Botul"—"nullified"—by the majority of the kosher pieces, i.e. it has lost its individuality, its individual specific characteristics. This, however, only applies when the object of the "nullification" consists of something that is sold by *weight* such as meat. If however, a treyfa egg, for example, becomes mixed up amongst kosher eggs, then even if there be a thousand eggs, they are all unfit for eating, for we cannot tell which one is treyfa. We cannot say, in this case, that the egg has become "Botul," because an egg is sold by number, (by the dozen) and it is a general principle in Torah Law that an item sold by number (which shows its individual importance[3]) does not become "Botul." In other words, the fact that a group is counted makes it clear that each unit of this group is considered to have a special value and distinctiveness and cannot become "Botul" or "null."

The significance of counting the Jewish people is now clear. Although the census of the people reveals nothing about the qualities of any one individual Jew as compared to his fellow, yet the very fact that G-d wanted them counted and numbered shows the worthiness and importance of the Jewish people individually and collectively.

REFERENCES:
    Based on Likuttei Sichos Vol. II p. 293.
        1) Numbers 1:2.
        2) Sotah 36b.
        3) Orlah cap. 3, Mishnah 7; Beitsa 3b and references ibid; Yorah Deah 110.
From "Within the complex..." until ... "Botul or Null." is the writer's explanation.

Sidra Shelach

WHO IS A JEW?

Having discussed last week the unique quality and nature of the Jew (as shown by G-d's command to *count* each individual) we bring in this regard a letter from the Lubavitcher Rebbe א״טילש to Mr. David Ben Gurion (the then Prime Minister of Israel) on the question of "Who is a Jew?"

His Excellency,
Mr. David Ben-Gurion,
Prime Minister of Israel.
Greetings:

This is in reply to your letter regarding my opinion on the Registration of children of mixed marriages, when the father is a Jew and the mother a non-Jew who did not undergo conversion before the birth of the child. The intent of the inquiry is—as the wording of the resolution has it in the above mentioned letter—"to define instructions that should be in harmony with the tradition accepted in all circles of Judaism, both orthodox and non-orthodox of all trends, and with the special conditions of Israel as a Sovereign State which guarantees freedom of conscience and religion as a center of ingathering the exiles."

My opinion is absolutely clear, in conformity with the Torah and the tradition accepted for generations, that in these matters there can be no validity whatsoever to a verbal declaraion expressing the desire to register as a Jew. Such a declaration has no power to change the reality.

According to the Torah and the tradition of ages which still exists today, a Jew is only a person born of a Jewish mother; or a proselyte who had been converted in conformity with the exact procedure laid down in the authoritative codes of Judaism from ancient times down to the Shulchan Aruk.

The above applies not only to children whose parents or guardians declare their desire to register them as Jews, but to whosoever comes forward to declare his wish to change his status in order to enter the Jewish community. Such a declaration has no force whatever unless he actually fulfills, or has fulfilled the appropriate conversion procedure as laid down in the Jewish codes in the Shulchan Aruk, *as above.*

                    With honor and blessing,

I do not cite sources since there are clear and detailed rulings on the matter in the codes of Maimonides, the Tur, Shulchan Aruk, *etc.*

                              Menachem Mendel Schneerson

All that follows now is merely an additional postscript, written with the intention of emphasizing that even if the following is not accepted, either in part or in full, this does not detract at all from the finality of the opinion I have outlined above. The following remarks are merely a reaction to the account of the situation delineated in your letter.

a) The question of registration, or however it may be described, is not a matter confined to Israel alone. It goes without saying — as explained in your letter — that no one may raise a barrier between the Jews of Israel and those of the Diaspora. On the contrary, all our brethren, wherever they may be, have constituted one people, from the moment of their emergence, in spite of their dispersion in all the corners of the world. Consequently the solution of the problem must be one that is acceptable to all members of the Jewish people everywhere, that is capable of forging and strengthening the bonds of unity between all Jews, and certainly not one that would be cause, even the remotest, of disunity and dissension. Accordingly, even if you may argue that the present conditions in Eretz Israel call for a special study of the above-mentioned question, these conditions do not restrict the problem to Eretz Israel, but, as noted, constitute a matter of common concern to every Jew everywhere.

b) The belonging to the Jewish people was never considered by our people as a formal, external matter. It has always been defined and delineated in terms of the committment of the whole being of the Jew, something intimately linked with his very essence and innermost experience. Accordingly, any movement which disregards or belittles any of the procedures in this connection degrades the feeling of belonging to the Jewish people and cannot but be detrimental to the serious and profound attitude towards the Jew's inner link with his people.

c) To ease the conditions of transition and affiliation to the Jewish people—particularly in the special circumstances of Eretz Israel, surrounded by countries and peoples unsympathetic towards it (that is an understatement)—is to endanger considerably the security of Eretz Israel.

d) What emerges from the above points is that even if an attempt is made to avoid the proper solution to the problem by a compromise, such as substituting for the word "Jew" a word of completely secular connotations, this will not constitute a way out, since the damage would remain both with respect to strengthening the bonds of unity with Jews everywhere, as well as from the point of view of inner strength and security.

e) Of course, no argument can be adduced from the cases of persons who have been converted in the proper manner and have nevertheless caused harm to the Jewish people; on the other hand, there is the possibility that one who merely makes a verbal declaration of his Jewishness may benefit the Jewish people. The demand for a due conversion procedure is likewise not negated by the fact that there are "non-Jewish saints" who, as the description implies, are for all that, still "non-Jews."

f) In the frame of reference in which the question was put, the matter of discrimination was mentioned. Discrimination can, however, only apply to granting or withholding of rights, or meting out punishments; it can have no relevance to the question of Registration which has to do with existing reality.

Let me conclude with the hope and expectation that Eretz Israel in all its aspects, both present and future, should constitute a factor uniting Jews everywhere both orthodox and non-orthodox of all trends, by attuning itself in all its affairs more and more to the name by which it is known among all the peoples of the world—"the Holy Land."

Yours truly,

M. M. S.

Sidra Korach

A MEZUZA ON THE DOOR

This week's Sidra relates how Korach, a member of the priestly tribe of Levi, rebelliously challenged the leadership of Moses and the high priesthood of Aaron.

The Midrash relates that Korach confronted Moses with several questions.[1] One of them concerned a Mezuza. According to Torah law every house must have affixed on its right doorpost, a Mezuza, a small scroll of parchment containing the first two paragraphs of the *Shma Yisroel*. Korach demanded of Moses: "Does a house filled with scrolls of the Torah require a Mezuza?" Moses replied that the contents of the house were immaterial; a "Mezuza" was required on every doorpost.

* * *

What is the logic of Moses' reply to Korach? A Mezuza, after all, contains only two portions of the Torah. Why indeed should a house full of scrolls of the entire Torah require a Mezuza? And what if one has a Mezuza in a beautifully ornamented case lying on his shelf; why is this not good enough? What is the significance of having a Mezuza nailed to the *doorpost?*

The answer is that although the bookshelves of a house may be filled with Torah scrolls or other holy books, this may not ensure the religious behavior of its inhabitants. It is the Mezuza on the door which symbolizes the active awareness of G-d's presence. The Mezuza is placed on the doorpost,[2] where one enters

71

his home and leaves it. Symbolically, he takes its teachings of G-d with him wherever he goes. His Torah is not consigned to a bookshelf, to a place of study alone, to an intellectual exercise. It is a factor in his life at all times, and all his actions are guided by the realization that . . . "The L-rd our G-d is One,"[3] as written in the Mezuza.

* * *

We are told of someone boasting to his Rabbi about all the Torah he had learned and mastered. The Rabbi replied, "You tell only of the Torah that you have learned, but what has the Torah taught you? Ask not, 'How much Torah knowledge have I acquired?' Ask rather, 'How much has Torah trained, educated and refined me?' "

REFERENCES:
  Based on Likuttei Sichos Vol. 4 pp. 1316-18.
    1) Midrash Rabah beginning of Korach; Tanchumah Ibid.
    2) See also Maimonides, end of Hilchos Mezuzah; Tur Yoreh Deah 285.
    3) Deutronomy 6:4.

UNWARRANTED LOVE

During the "Three Weeks" between the 17th of Tammuz and the 9th of Av (the Fast Day—"Tisha B'Av") we mourn the "Churban Habayis", the destruction of the Beis Hamikdosh (the Sanctuary in Jerusalem) which took place in this season.

What is the purpose of remembering the "Churban Habayis"? It is not to evoke sadness or melancholy, nor is it mere commemoration. We are to understand the reason for the Destruction, and then apply that understanding in our daily lives. The Talmud tells us[1] that the Beis Hamikdosh was destroyed because of "Unwarranted Hatred" (Sinas Chinom) among our people, and it is this undesirable factor that we must attempt to remove from our daily lives. Unreasoning hatred is corrected through "unwarranted love" (Ahavas Chinom).

*　　*　　*

This Shabbos is the Chassidic festival of "Yud Beis Tammuz" (Tammuz 12th). Chassidim mark this day because in 1927 the late Lubavitcher Rebbe was released from Communist imprisonment, and it was his birthday as well. Many years before, on his Bar Mitzva day, the Rebbe asked[2] his father (who was the Lubavitcher Rebbe at that time), "Why do we say 'I hereby accept upon myself the positive commandment of Love Your Neighbor As Yourself,' each day before the morning prayers? What is the connection between this custom and prayer?"

His father replied: "In prayer a Jew asks G-d to grant him his needs. Before a child makes a request of his father, he tries to please him; the greatest pleasure

73

that a father can have is to see his children living together in peace and friendship. The Almighty is the Heavenly Father of all, young and old, rich and poor, learned and simple. When He sees all His children, with all their widely different and even clashing personalities, living together in unity and harmony[3] with brotherly love for each other, He grants the requests they make in prayer."

* * *

Ahavas Chinom means that we must show love to others regardless of past or anticipated kindnesses, even to one we have never seen! He may have no obvious qualities or virtues to warrant love. Still, Ahavas Chinom demands that we treat him with affection. When Israel dwells in friendship and harmony, united by the bond of Ahavas Chinom, they merit the speedy rebuilding of the fallen Beis Hamikdosh.

REFERENCES:
Based on Likuttei Sichos Vol. II pp. 597-9.
1) Yomah 9 b.
2) Sefer Hasichos Kayitz Tof-Shin p. 156.
3) Likkutei Diburim p. 565.

74

Sidra Pinchas

THE STORY OF A 'NIGUN'

Song and melody occupy a prominent place in the Chassidic way of life. Since the essence of Chassidism lies in a denial of pessimism and in the precept to serve G-d with joy and gladness of heart and with longing for communion with the Divine, melody is exalted as the means by which to dispel the gloom of despair and to replace it with the brightness of a joyful heart. The early leaders of Chassidism therefore either composed, or encouraged others to compose, melodies replete with emotional overtones. Sometimes these composers and singers detected a "holy spark" in the folk songs of the countries in which they lived, principally Bessarabia and the Ukraine, and integrated these motifs into their own music. This explains why Chassidic songs are sometimes sung in foreign languages.

About twelve years after the passing of the Baal Shem Tov (the founder of Chassidism) there arose a new light of Chassidism in the Jewish world, known as CHaBaD, from the initial letters of the words *Chochmo* (wisdom), *Bino* (understanding), and *Daas* (Knowledge), which indicate the intellectual principles upon which it was based. While Chabad Chassidism drew from the fountainhead of the Baal Shem Tov's philosophy, it developed its own flavor and characteristics. Rabbi Shneur Zalman of Liadi, known as the *Alter Rebbe,* founder of the Chabad movement, deepened and broadened the content of Chassidism; he also discovered new depths in Chassidic song. The Baal Shem Tov had revivified song itself in Jewish life; the Alter Rebbe revealed the inner soul of Chassidic melody.

Chabad melody differs considerably from general Chassidic song. It is not only joyous and ecstatic; it is reflective and mystical, with a pensive and yearning quality. An example of a Chabad 'Nigun' (melody)

75

with a profound moral and story is "Shamil's Nigun", which has the following background:

More than a century ago, there lived a leader of the Georgian tribes in Russia who then inhabited the Caucasus mountains. His name was Shamil. The Russian army engaged the Georgians in battle, seeking to conquer them and deprive them of their freedom. The Georgians fought valiantly against the invaders and could not be beaten. The Russian army leaders then proposed a false peace treaty and by this means succeeded in getting the Georgians to lay down their arms. Immediately afterwards, however, the Russians lured the Georgian leader, Shamil, away from his stronghold and confined him to prison.

Staring out of the window of his small, narrow cell, Shamil reflected on his days of liberty in the past. In his current exile and helplessness, he bewailed his plight and yearned for his previous position of freedom and fortune. He consoled himself, however, with the knowledge that he would eventually be released from his imprisonment and he would return to his previous position with even more power and glory. It is the above thought that is expressed in this melancholy, yearning, yet ultimately hopeful 'nigun'.

The Moral: The soul descends to this world from the heavens above, clothed in the earthly body of a human being. The soul's physical vestments here are really its prison cell, for it constantly longs for spiritual, heavenly fulfillment. The soul strives to free itself from the "exile" of the human body and its earthly pleasures by directing its physical being into the paths of Torah and Mitzvos.

* * *

The musical notes for 'Shamil's Nigun' are printed overleaf. As a follow-up to this introduction to the world of Chassidic song, various Chabad melodies will appear from time to time on the back pages of this publication.

THE COINS SHONE

This week's Sidra makes prominent mention of the daughters of Tzelofchod,[1] who were wise[2] and righteous[3] women. Their tradition has been faithfully and magnificently continued by Jewish women through the generations. A Chassidic story is apropos:

Reb Gavriel, a Chosid of the Alter Rebbe, and his wife, Chana Rivka, had been married for twenty-five years, but were childless. He had been a prosperous merchant in Vitebsk, but hard times and persecution had destroyed Reb Gavriel's fortune. The Alter Rebbe was at that time trying to arrange for the release of some Jewish prisoners. Large sums of ransom money were needed, which the Rebbe attempted to raise amongst his followers. Reb Gavriel was "estimated" as being able to donate a certain sum—but he could not; he was heart-broken at not being able to participate in the great Mitzva of "Pidyon Shevuyim" (Redemption of Captives) to the extent expected of him.

On learning of her husband's distress, his wife sold her pearls and jewelry for the required sum of money. She then scoured and polished the coins till they sparkled, and with a heartfelt prayer that their fortune should also begin to shine, she packed up the coins and gave them to Reb Gavriel to bring to the Rebbe.

When he came to the Alter Rebbe in Liozna, Reb Gavriel placed the package in front of the Rebbe on the table. At the Rebbe's request he opened the package; the coins shone with an extraordinary brilliance. The Alter Rebbe became pensive, lost in thought for a few moments. Then he said, "Of all the gold, silver and copper which the Jews gave to build the Mishkan (the desert sanctuary) nothing shone but the brass-laver and its stand. (These were made from the copper cosmetic mirrors which the Jewish women had selflessly and joyously given to the Mishkan)[4]. "Tell me," continued the Rebbe, "where did you get these coins?" Reb Gavriel told the Rebbe of his plight and how his wife Chana Rivka had raised the money.

The Alter Rebbe rested his head on his hand, and was lost for a long while in profound thought. Then, raising his head, he blessed Reb Gavriel and his wife with children, long years, riches and extraordinary grace. He told Reb Gavriel to close his business in Vitebsk and to deal with diamonds and precious stones. The blessing was wholly fulfilled. Reb Gavriel 'Nossay Cheyn' (the 'graceful')—as he came to be called— became a wealthy man and the father of sons and daughters. He died at the age of 110 years and was outlived by his wife by two years!

*   *   *

The "coins of charity" (material or spiritual charity) may be the same as ordinary coins in number and in value, but when the Mitzva is done with self-sacrifice—yet with *joy*—it acquires an inestimably greater value, and shines with a brilliance that illuminates one's whole life.

REFERENCES:
    Based on Likuttei Sichos Vol. IV p. 1300.
      1) Numbers Cap. 36.
      2) See Rashi on Numbers 27:4.
      3) Ibid 27:1.
      4) Exodus 38:8 and see Rashi Ibid.

Sidra Devorim

A LETTER OF CONSOLATION

This Shabbos is "Shabbos Chazon," the Shabbos preceding the fast day of Tisha B'Av, when we mourn the destruction of the Beis Hamikdosh, the Sanctuary in Jerusalem. We bring you a free translation and adaptation of a letter of condolence written by the Lubavitcher Rebbe שליט״א to one of the renowned generals of Israel's army in the Six-Day War.

Greeting and Blessing!

I was deeply distressed to hear of your great loss — the tragic death of your young son, may be rest in peace.

It is not given to us to know the ways of the Creator. During the war, during the time of danger, it was His will that all be saved. Indeed you, sir, were one of those who achieved victory for our people of Israel against our enemies, when the many were delivered into the hands of the few. Yet, at home, and during a time of peace, this terrible tragedy happened! But how can a mortal understand the ways of the Creator? There is no comparing our minds and His. We do not wonder that a small child does not understand the ways and conduct of an old and wise man, though the difference between them is only relative.

This is no attempt to minimize the extent of your pain and grief, and I, too, share in your sorrow, though I am so far from you.

* * *

Even in such a great tragedy as this, solace can be found in the words of our traditional expression of consolation to mourners—an expression which has become hallowed by the law and tradition of many generations of our people. "May the Almighty comfort you among the other mourners of Zion and Jerusalem." We may ask, why mention those who mourn for "Zion and Jerusalem" when comforting an individual on his personal loss? A deeper analysis will, however, reveal that the mourner will find comfort precisely in this comparison of his loss with the Destruction and exile of Zion, for several reasons.

79

First, the mourning over the Destruction of Zion and Jerusalem is shared by Jews the world over. It is true that those who live in Jerusalem and actually see the Western Wall and our Beis Hamikdosh in ruins feel the anguish more deeply, but even those who live far away feel sorrow. Similarly, the grief-stricken individual or family will find solace in the thought that "all the children of Israel are as one complete whole"[1],that their sorrow is shared by all our people.

Second, we have perfect confidence that G-d will rebuild the ruins of Zion and Jerusalem; He will gather the dispersed remnants of Israel from the ends of the earth through our righteous Moshiach, and bring them in gladness to witness the joy of Zion and Jerusalem. We are equally confident that G-d will fulfill His promise that ". . . the dwellers of dust (the dead) shall awake and give praise."[2] Great indeed will be the happiness and rejoicing then, when all will meet together after the Revival of the Dead.

Third, the Babylonians and the Romans were able to destroy only the Beis Hamikdosh of wood and stone, of gold and silver, but they could not harm the inner "Beis Hamikdosh" in the heart of every Jew, for it is eternal. In the very same way, the hand of death can touch only the body, but the soul is eternal; it has simply ascended to the World of Truth. Every good deed we do in accordance with the will of G-d, the Giver of life, adds to the merit of the departed soul, as well as to its spiritual welfare.

May it be G-d's will that you and your family know no more pain and distress. May you find true comfort and solace in your communal endeavors, defending the Holy Land, the land ". . . . over which G-d your L-rd watches from the beginning of the year until the end of the year"[3], as well as in those endeavors of your private life—observing the Mitzva of Tefillin, one Mitzva bringing another, and yet another, in its train.[4]

REFERENCES:
Based on a letter of the Lubavitcher Rebbe שליט"א dated Tishrei 13, 5728.

1) Likuttei Torah, Nitsovim (beginning).
2) Isa. 26:19.
3) Deuteronomy 11:12.
4) See Pirkei Avos 4:2.

CHARITY AT HOME

This week's Sidra contains the familiar "Shma Yisroel", the prayer said three times daily. One of the verses in this prayer is: "And you shall teach them (the words of the Torah) to your children . . ."[1]

* * *

The Talmud relates[2] that the great sage Abba Chilkiya and his wife were both charitable, yet, when they both prayed for rain at a time of drought, *her* prayers were answered before her husband's. The explanation is that Abba Chilkiya gave money to the needy, with which to buy food. His wife, however, gave the food itself, not merely the means with which to buy food. For this thoughtfulness her prayers were answered before her husband's.

* * *

Charity is not limited to material assistance; it extends to supplying the spiritual needs of another. For example, ensuring the correct Jewish education and upbringing of one's children—(for charity is not only helping a stranger, but even one's own family[3]) is no less "Tsedaka" than feeding and clothing them. In this form of charity too, we find that the father provides the *means,* but the mother gives the child the (spiritual) food itself.

Every Jewish father is commanded by G-d ". . . you shall teach them to your children."[2] Yet most fathers do not directly teach their children. The fathers engage a teacher or a Jewish school to do it for them, and the fathers fulfill their Mitzva indirectly.

The "Alter Rebbe", founder of Chabad Chassidism, once said to a Chassid, "I am obliged to fulfill the Mitzva of 'And you shall teach them to your children'.

You are obliged to fulfill the Mitzva of supporting your family. Let us exchange. I will give you the financial means to fulfill *your* Mitzva and you help me observe *my* Mitzva by teaching my Berel." The Chassid taught his young son Dov Ber, who later became the famed "Mitteler Rebbe", the second Rebbe in the Chabad dynasty.[4]

In the father's "giving charity" to his child, he does not supply the actual spiritual sustenance, but only the preparation for it. He pays the teacher, and the teacher instructs the child. On the other hand the mother provides the spiritual nourishment itself. She must see to it that the little boy wears a *Tallis Koton* (four-cornered garment with 'Tsitsis'—fringes) at all times, that the child laves his hands at the bedside ("Negel Vasser"), that he pronounces Brochos before eating or drinking, and so on. For even a child who studies in a cheder, Yeshiva or day-school might frustrate all his teachers' efforts by neglecting to implement at home the Judaism he has absorbed in school. It is the mother who must guard against this possibility and train the child in correct Torah conduct, and, like Abba Chilkiya's wife, *she* earns the "rains" of blessing and success for her entire family.

REFERENCES:
  Based on Likuttei Sichos Vol. II p. 580.
    1) Deuteronomy 6:7.
    2) Taanis 23b.
    3) Kesubos 50a: "He who sustains and supports his own young sons and daughters is considered as continually fulfilling the Mitzva of Tsedaka."
    4) Hayom Yom, 8 Adar I. See also "Thoughts" Vol. I p. 106.

LEARN TORAH, LOVE TORAH

In this week's Sidra, Eikev, we are commanded to teach the Torah to our children and to discuss and study Torah —"When you sit in your house, and when you walk by the way, and when you lie down, and when you arise."[1]

* * *

"Hillel will cause the poor to be found guilty; Rabbi Eliezer Ben Charsum will cause the rich to be found guilty."[2] So say the sages of the Talmud, giving the following explanation: At the final judgment when the soul stands before the heavenly court, one of the questions put to him is, "Why did you not study Torah?" The reply may be, "I was poor and too busy trying to make a living; I had no time to study Torah." This answer will be rejected by the court, for he was certainly no poorer than Hillel who used to work for half a day and earn a trifling half-dinar. He would give half of this coin to the doorkeeper of the Torah study-hall to be allowed to listen to the discourse of the two great Rabbis and scholars Shmaya and Avtalyon. The other half of his wages would go for his family and himself.

The Talmud tells us[3] that one wintry day Hillel found no work, and being unable to pay for entrance to the Beis Hamedrash, he climbed onto the roof and lay down with his ear to the skylight window to hear some precious Torah-learning, not realizing that it had started to snow heavily. The next morning Shmaya remarked to Avtalyon that the room was strangely dark. They looked up and saw the shape of a body over the skylight. Rushing up to the roof, they found Hillel frozen stiff under more than four feet of snow! Apparently Hillel did not permit poverty to deter him.

Another excuse offered the heavenly court might be, "I was a man of affairs. My time was completely taken up in running my business. I had no time to study Torah". This answer is also rejected, for the accused was certainly no wealthier than Rabbi Eliezer Ben Charsum who inherited a thousand townships and a thousand ships at sea, yet he went from town to town and from country to country to study Torah, carrying his frugal provisions on his back. Wealth was no obstacle for Rabbi Eliezer.

* * *

Let us probe the reasoning behind the guilty verdict in the two cases. If the accused really had time to study Torah and neglected to do so, there is no need to bring proof of their guilt from Hillel or Rabbi Eliezer. If, on the other hand, they really had no time for Torah study, then why are they guilty?

The answer is that a Jew should have a compelling, burning love for Torah, for it is G-d's precious gift to us, His people. Granted, there are times that we are exempt (according to the strict letter of Jewish law) from studying Torah, but even then we should be driven to take a few precious moments to learn G-d's Torah. The challenge of the heavenly court is not so much, "Why did you not study the Torah as prescribed by G-d's law?" but rather "Where was your *love* for Torah that would have impelled you to study it even when exempt from doing so, as did Hillel and Rabbi Eliezer?"

REFERENCES:
Based on Likuttei Sichos Vol. II p. 304.
1) Deuternomy 11:19.
2) Yomah 35 b.
3) Ibid.

TORAH AND HEREDITY

The opening words of this week's Sidra are: "Behold I set before you this day a blessing and a curse. The blessing, if you will heed the commandments of the L-rd etc. . . . and the curse, if you will not heed the commandments etc."[1] When a Jew turns away, G-d forbid, from the path of Torah and Mitzvos, this, in itself, is a curse.

* * *

The importance of heredity in transmitting physical, mental, and spiritual characteristics is well known and obvious, even in the case of several generations. How much more so where a trait is transmitted and intensified over the course of many generations uninterruptedly, when such a trait becomes part of the very essence of the individual, his very nature.

It is also clear that when a person—as in the case of all living things—wishes to change an inborn trait which is deeply rooted in him, not to mention something that touches his essential nature, it would demand tremendous efforts; the outcome is bound to be destructive rather than constructive, creating a terrible upheaval in him, with most unfortunate results.

I have in mind particularly the Jew, man and woman, who, belonging to one of the oldest nations in the world with a recorded history of over thirty-five hundred years, is naturally and innately bound up with the Jewish people with every fiber of his life and soul. Hence, such sects or groups which tried to depart from the true Jewish way of life of the Torah and Mitzvos, could not survive, as history has amply demonstrated. Such dissident groups uprooted themselves from their natural soil and far from being constructive, became the worst enemies of the Jewish people and their worst persecutors.

Only Jews who have faithfully adhered to the Torah and Mitzvos, as they were revealed on Mount Sinai, have survived all their persecutors, for only through the Torah and Mitzvos can the Jewish people attach themselves to the Supreme Power, G-d, who has given us the Torah and our way of life.

* * *

If we reflect on this, we will come to cherish the great and sacred knowledge which has been handed down to us, generation after generation, from the revelation at Mount Sinai to the present day. Accepting this sacred tradition unconditionally and without questions does not mean that there is no room for any intellectual understanding. Within our limitations there is a great deal that we can understand, for G-d in His infinite grace has given us insights into some aspects of His commandments, insights which grow deeper with our practising the Mitzvos in our daily lives and making them our daily experience. In this way the Jew attains true peace of mind and a harmonious and happy life, not only spiritually but also physically, and fully realizes how fortunate he is to be a son or daughter of this great and holy nation,[2] our Jewish people.

REFERENCES:
　　Based on a letter of the Lubavitcher Rebbe שליט״א dated Teves 11, 5718.
　　1) Deuteronomy 11: 26-28.
　　2) Exodus 19:6.

Sidra Shofetim

INNER FAITH, NOT *INTER*-FAITH (Part 1)

The month of Elul has just begun. Elul is the month of "Teshuvah" (repentance), a time for serious introspection by every Jew as to his attitudes, views and beliefs. We bring in this regard two excerpts (Part 1 this week and Part 2 next week) of a letter by the Lubavitcher Rebbe, שליט״א in reply to the question, "What should be the Jewish attitude to "interfaith dialogue."

* * *

... In reply to your question as to what should be the Jewish attitude towards the matter of "religious dialogue" which has been advocated in certain Jewish and non-Jewish circles.

It surprises me that you should have any doubt in this matter. For, anyone with some knowledge of Jewish history knows with what reluctance Jews viewed religious debates with non-Jews. There were many good reasons for this attitude, in addition to the basic reason that Jews do not consider it their mission to convert gentiles to their faith, nor do they wish to expose themselves to the missionary zeal of other faiths.

Each and every generation has its own characteristics which have a bearing on contemporary problems. One of the peculiarities of our own day and age—a circumstance which makes such "dialogue" even more reprehensible—is the confusion and perplexity which are so widespread now, especially among the younger generation. Symptomatic of this confusion is the lowering, or even toppling, of the once well-defined boundaries in various areas of the daily life. This process, which began with the lowering, or abolishing altogether, of the Mechitzah in the synagogue, has extended itself also to the abolishing of boundaries in the areas of ethics, morality, and even common decency. In some quarters it has even led to a perversion of values, reminiscent of the lament of the prophet: "Woe unto them that call evil good, and good evil; that put darkness for light, and light for darkness; that put bitter for sweet, and sweet for bitter!" (Isaiah 5:20).

One can hardly blame the young generation for their confusion and perplexity, considering the upheavals, revolutions and wars which have plagued our times, and the bankruptcies of the various systems and ideologies to which the young generation has pinned its hopes for a better world. Moreover, many of those who should have been the teachers and guides of the younger generation, have compounded the confusion and misdirection, for various reasons which need not be elaborated here.

One of the consequences of the said state of affairs is also the misconception prevailing in some quarters regarding the so-called "interfaith" movement. The "brotherhood of man-

kind" is a positive concept only so long as it is confined to such areas as commerce, philanthropy, and various civil and economic aspects of the society, wherein peoples of various faiths and minority groups must live together in harmony, mutual respect and dignity. Unfortunately, the concept of "brotherhood" has been misconstrued to require members of one faith to explain their religious beliefs and practices to members of another faith, and in return to receive instruction in the religion of others. Far from clarifying matters, these inter-faith activities have, at best, added to the confusion, and, at worst, have been used with missionary zeal by those religions which are committed to proselytizing members of other faiths.

The alarmingly growing rate of intermarriage has a variety of underlying causes. But there can be no doubt that one of the factors is the interfaith movement, or "dialogue" (which is a euphemism for the same), wherein clergymen of one faith are invited to preach from the pulpit of another. It is easy to see what effect this has on the minds of the young, as well as of their parents, whose commitments to their own faith are in any case near the vanishing point.

This in itself offers a complete justification for the prohibition which the Torah imposes upon the study of other faiths — if, indeed, external justification were necessary. Only in exceptional cases does the Torah permit the study of other religions, and that also only to specially qualified persons. Bitter experience has made it abundantly clear how harmful any such interfaith or dialogue is. Thus, even those Jews to whom the Torah is not yet, unfortunately, their Pillar of Light to illuminate their life, but who still wish to preserve their Jewish identity and, especially, the Jewish identity of their children—even they should clearly see the dangers of intermarriage and complete assimilation, G-d forbid, lurking behind these so-called "dialogues," and should reject them in no uncertain terms.

While we must not give up a single Jewish soul which happens to be in danger of straying from the path of Torah and Mitsvoth, and certainly in danger of intermarriage, or assimilation, G-d forbid, and we must spare no effort in trying to save that Jew or Jewess, even if it involves a lengthy "dialogue" with him or her, we must just as resolutely reject any such dialogue with a non-Jew, for the reasons mentioned, and also because we have no interest in his conversion to our faith.

To be sure, we have obligations to our society at large. We must contribute our share to the common weal, help to maintain and raise the standards of morality and ethics, and to encourage the non-Jew to observe the "Seven Precepts of the Children of Noah" in all their ramifications. But to accomplish these objectives, there is no need for us whatever to have any religious dialogues with non-Jews, nor any interfaith activities in the form of religious discussions, interchange of pulpits, and the like.

(To be Continued)

INNER FAITH, NOT *INTER*-FAITH (Part 2)

The following is the second of two excerpts of a letter by the Lubavitcher Rebbe שליט״א on the subject of "interfaith dialogue".

. . . Furthermore, I wish to stress the following points:—

(1) In most polemics, debates, dialogues and the like, the usual outcome is not a rapprochement of minds and hearts; rather do they evoke an impulse of rivalry and the desire to score a point, or gain a victory over the opponent by any means. This is usually the case even in non-religious polemics, and certainly very much so in religious debates, inasmuch as the subject matter touches one's inner soul; and even more so where religious zealots are concerned.

Hence, if the purpose of the "dialogue" is a rapprochement, it is doomed from the start, and often even brings the opposite results.

(2) Where one party to the dialogue is committed to proselytizing, and the other is not, it is clear that the dialogue will be used by the first to accomplish its purpose, and the "dialogue" will in effect become a "monologue".

(3) Looking at the question from a practical standpoint, perhaps the most important point is that the effort expended on such "dialogues" is, to say the least, a waste we can ill afford. For, every individual has only limited resources of time, energy, and influence, while every right-thinking person must feel a sense of responsibility to accomplish something in behalf of the community in which he lives. Experience has shown that the benefits, if any, from all such "dialogues" in terms of a better understanding among men of different faiths and races, have been hardly discernable. But certain it is that the energies thus expended have been at the expense of vital areas of Yiddishkeit, where there is a crying need for strengthening the Jewish faith and practices within our own ranks, especially among the younger generation.

There are, of course, some well-meaning, but misguided individuals, who see in interfaith and dialogue an avenue of lofty goals and ideals deserving of their utmost efforts. But there are also those who encourage them in their misconceptions, thus abetting the misdirection and misplacement of energies and resources, sorely needed elsewhere, namely, and to repeat, in the spreading among our youths, a deeper knowledge of the Torah, Torath Chayim, *which, as the name indicates, is the true guide in the daily life of the Jew, at all times, and in all places. For the Torah's truths are eternal, having been given by the Eternal, the Creator of man, and*

*the Master and Ruler of the World, at all times and all places.
It is a tragic irony, that precisely in this day and age, and in
this country, where we have been blessed with freedom of
worship, and do not face persecution and constant peril for
every observance as in certain less fortunate countries, yet
so many of our younger generation are lost to us daily by the
default, negligence and misdirection of the leaders who should
know better.*

*It is high time to replace interfaith with inner-faith, and
concentrate on dialogue with our own misguided youth, as
well as—to our shame — with the adults, so as to fan their
slumbering embers of faith and to illuminate their lives with
the Pillar of Light and the Pillar of Fire of the Torah.*

With blessing,
signed: MENACHEM SCHNEERSON

*P.S. In order to bring my reply in fuller accord with the
details of your question, the above has been couched in terms
that would be fitting for a person who is not committed to the
Shulchan Aruch (Code of Jewish Law). However, from the
viewpoint of the Jew to whom the Torah is indeed "a lamp
unto his feet," the true guide and illumination in his daily
life, the decisive reason for the outright rejection of religious
dialogue is the prohibition imposed by the Torah against the
study of other religions, except in very specific cases and by
specially qualified individuals, as already mentioned.*

*In this connection I wish to clarify one more point. It is
sometimes argued that the rejection of religious dialogue, or
the prohibition of the study of other religions, indicates an
acknowledgement of weakness, G-d forbid, on the part of the
Torah vis-a-vis other religions. There is no need to refute this
fallacious argument. However, if a weakness is involved, it
is that of human nature. In the face of a promise of an easier
way of life, free from the restrictions of 248 positive and 365
negative precepts, and more freedom to gratify one's lower
instincts, many an individual may succumb to the temptation. Moreover, the human mind is often so inconstant that
one may readily overlook the most glaring and evident truths
that bar the way to the gratification of one's lusts.*

*Besides, in any dialogue or debate, the victory often goes
not to the proponent of the truth, but to the one who is more
skilled in dialectic and oratory. By sheer rhetoric, by the gift
of eloquence, one may even succeed in calling "evil good and
darkness light" to which reference has been made in the beginning of this letter.*

*Thus, from whatever viewpoint you consider the matter,
religious dialogue with non-Jews has no place in Jewish life,
least of all here and now.*

PRACTICE WHAT YOU PREACH

The 18th Elul falls this week, the birthday of Rabbi Shneur Zalman of Liadi, founder of Chabad Chassidism. It is also the birthday of the Baal Shem Tov, founder of the general Chassidic movement. It is no wonder that this day acquired a special significance among Chassidim. Special meaning was read into the number "eighteen", so popular because its Hebrew equivalent spells "Chai" (alive), and this day became known as "Chai Elul."

* * *

The moral person must strive to bring his personal life and daily conduct in full harmony with his convictions, to actually live up to the standards of morality and ethics which he has set himself. This is particularly true of the Jewish religious person, since the Jewish religion is a way of everyday life, and considers the deed, the daily conduct, as the ultimate purpose of knowledge.

Studying the life of Rabbi Shneur Zalman (known as the "Alter Rebbe"), the exponent of the Chassidic teachings of the Baal Shem Tov and founder of Chabad, one marvels at the complete accord between his personal life and his philosophy and teachings. He was the living embodiment of all that he taught and more. He was a person of many accomplishments, even down to matters of small detail—for he strove to develop himself in every way.

His every act was careful and deliberate, executed in a meticulous fashion. Making "Ahavas Yisroel", love of one's fellow Jew—in its immediate application in actual practice—a cornerstone of his ethical system, he missed no opportunity of applying it in his own life. Once he received five thousand gold coins, a most sub-

91

stantial sum, and immediately he dedicated it all to a fund for needy families.

He was the 'Baal Koreh', reading the Torah in his congregation, giving particular attention to pronunciation and grammatical rules; he was also the 'Baal Tokeah', sounding the shofar on Rosh Hashana. In composing his 'Shulchan Aruch' (code of Jewish law) he personally checked the weights and measures defined by Jewish law. He studied algebra, geometry and astronomy in order to avoid relying on others in making calculations essential to the study of the Talmud and making legal decisions. Knowing the value of melody in the attainment of religious devotion, he himself composed melodies and sang them. Meticulous in all his ways, he sifted scores of prayer books (according to one tradition—no less than sixty different versions) before publishing his own Siddur.

The philosophy of the Alter Rebbe is fully reflected in his life story; his life was a living example of what he taught.

REFERENCES:
 Based on the foreword of the Lubavitcher Rebbe to "Rabbi Schneur Zalman of Liadi" by Dr. Nissan Mindel.
 We strongly recommend this excellent biography of our great sage, the Alter Rebbe.

THE ABSOLUTE TRUTH

Adaptation of excerpts of a letter to an individual by the Lubavitcher Rebbe שליט״א .

In the forthcoming weeks the closing Sidras of the Torah are being read. At this time it would be well to examine the Rabbinic saying, "The Torah spoke in the language of man".[1] Some interpret this as meaning that each segment of Jewry should be addressed in its own language and terms. Each community and congregation, they maintain, should be presented with a philosophy of Torah that has been adapted to their particular beliefs. This is a distortion. The principle of "The Torah spoke the language of man" applies only to the "language," the expression, leaving the content intact.

Our Torah is called "Toras Emes," the Torah of truth, because it is eternal, constant. When the truth is modified or altered by compromise, to whatever degree, it ceases to be the truth. The truth remains the same for all people at all times. If one accepts that the Torah was given by G-d, then he cannot say that "times have changed" and the Torah in its original form is no longer applicable. As if the Creator and Governor of the universe could not have foreseen that there would be a twentieth century!

In the 19th century it was the prevailing view of scientists that human reason was infallible in scientific deductions, and sciences like physics, chemistry and mathematics were absolute truths—not merely tested theories, but absolute facts. A new idolatry arose, not of wood and stone, but the worship of science. In the 20th century, however, and especially in recent decades, the whole complexion of science has changed. The assumed immutability of the scientific laws, the concept of absolutism in science generally, have been modified. The contrary view, known as the "principle of indeterminism" is now accepted. Nothing is *certain* any more in science, only *relative* or *probable*. Scientific findings are now presented with considerable reservation, with limited and temporary validity, in the expectation that they are likely to be replaced any day by a more advanced theory.

Living as we do in this climate of scientific uncertainty there is no reason to attempt to reconcile the uncertainties of scientific findings (which science itself declares as only "probable") with the eternal truth of the Torah which cannot be diluted or compromised.

REFERENCES:
1) Brochos 31 b.

Rosh Hashana

THE MONTH OF TISHREI

During the colorful month of Tishrei, every nuance of Jewish life finds expression—solemn days, fast days, and days of rejoicing. It is not coincidence that the first month of the year has "samples" of every shade and color of Jewish life, for these "samples" are intended as introduction and guidance for the entire year. By observing the special days of Tishrei in their proper spirit, we are initiated into a truly Jewish life, in accordance with the spirit of the Torah, for the coming year.

* * *

What can we learn from the special days of Tishrei?

a. Rosh Hashanah is the day that Adam, the first man, proclaimed G-d's sovereignty over Creation. When we embark on some endeavor, we must remember that G-d is the Creator of heaven and earth and the sole Ruler of the universe, and that our venture must have His approval. This is further emphasized by—

b. The Ten Days of Repentance which remind us that as servants of the King we must keep check on our deeds to ensure that they conform with the wishes of the Master. However, since we are only human, we are liable to fail on occasions. This is why G-d gives us—

c. Yom Kippur to impress upon us the realization that it is never too late to return, provided we do it sincerely, with remorse and rejection of our past misdeeds and solemn resolve to do better in the future. With this firm resolution, G-d forgives us, and cleanses us of our sins. Difficult though it may appear to change habits and practice unfamiliar disciplines—

d. Succos helps us not to despair in days of difficulty, for G-d is our protector. The Succah recalls the Clouds of Glory with which He surrounded us during the forty years' wandering through the desert after the departure from Egypt. Finally, in order to know how to lead our lives in accord with G-d's wishes we have—

e. Shemini Atzeres and Simchas Torah, the festivals of rejoicing in the *Torah*. In Torah G-d gave us Divine laws of justice and righteousness and a true guide in life. By conducting our lives accordingly, we are assured of true happiness in every sense. Torah is a "tree of life to them that hold fast to it, and its supporters are fortunate.'"

* * *

These, briefly, are some lessons of Tishrei. By following them faithfully, the New Year will be a happy one both spiritually and materially, and the blessing which we give each other, *Leshono Tovo Tikosev Vesaychosem*—"May you be written and inscribed for a good year,"—will surely be fulfilled.

REFERENCES:
    Based on a letter of the Lubavitcher Rebbe א״טילש
        1) Proverbs 3:18.

Sidra Ha'azinu; Shabbos Shuva

ASSETS OF TODAY'S YOUTH

This Shabbos is 'Shabbos Shuva', the Sabbath of Repentance. The 'Baal Teshuva', one who repents of his
previous way of life and turns to Torah and Mitzvos
faces up to a great challenge—the challenge of *chang-
ing* his entire previous way of thinking and his whole
pattern of conduct.

* * *

It is customary to find fault with the present generation by comparison with the preceding one. Whatever
conclusions one may arrive at from this comparison,
one thing is unquestionably true—that the new generation is not afraid to face a challenge; not only the kind
of challenge which places them at variance with the
majority, but even the kind of challenge which calls
for sacrifices and changes in their personal lives. Some
of our contemporary young people are quite prepared
to accept a challenge with all its consequences, while
others who may not, as yet, be ready to accept it for one
reason or another, at least show respect for those who
have accepted it, and also respect for the one who
brought them face to face with this challenge. This is
quite different from olden days, when it took a great
deal of courage to challenge prevailing opinions and
ideas; often a person who had the courage to do so was
branded as an impractical individual, a dreamer, and
so on.

What is more, many of our young people do not rest
content with taking up a challenge which has to do
only with a beautiful theory, or even a profound philosophy, but want also to hear about the practical application of such a theory not only as an occasional ex-

perience, but as a *daily* experience. In fact, this is the kind of theory which appeals to them most.

A further asset of our youth is their changed attitude towards the person who brings the challenge: We find that "Ba'alei Teshuva", individuals who have themselves but recently become committed to Torah-observance, make a deep and lasting impression upon any young people they talk to about Torah-Judaism. Even though it seems logical that the one who brings the challenge to the young people should have a background of many years of identification with, and personification of, the idea which he promulgates, this is no longer expected nowadays. We are used to seeing quick and radical changes at every step in the physical world, and if this is possible in the physical world, it is certainly possible in the realm of the spiritual, as our Sages declared regarding a 'Baal Teshuva': "A person may sometimes acquire an eternity in a single moment". Thus, no individual can ignore his duty to share his newly-won truth, even if he has no record of decades of identification with it. As a matter of fact, this may even be an added advantage, in that it can impress a precedent on others.

REFERENCES:
Adapted from a letter by the Lubavitcher Rebbe א״טילש dated Iyar 15, 5724.

"HAKHEL"—"GATHER THE PEOPLE"[1]

In the time of the Beis Hamikdosh (the Sanctuary in Jerusalem) there took place once every seven years during the days of Sukos a colorful ceremony known as "Hakhel". "Hakhel", which means "gather", required that all Jewish people—men, women and children, and even the very young ones, gather at the Beis Hamikdosh to listen to certain portions of the Torah read by the king.

Although the Beis Hamikdosh has been destroyed, Torah and Mitzvos are eternal. Hence, even those Mitzvos which were to be practised only at the time of the Beis Hamikdosh, by virtue of their eternal spiritual content, have a special significance in their appropriate time, which has to be expressed and fulfilled in an appropriate manner.

The Torah was given so that it should permeate and vitalize the daily life of every Jew—man, woman, and child, to the extent that their entire being become one of Torah and Mitzvos. In order to help attain this goal the Torah was read at the Hakhel ceremony by the *King,* whose awe-inspiring quality filled the audience with an overwhelming sense of subservience and self-effacement.

Such was the precept of 'Hakhel' in olden days. As for our own generation, the message of the Mitzvah of 'Hakhel' for each of us is that it calls upon us to utilize the opportune awe-inspiring days of the current month of Tishrei to gather our fellow Jews — man, woman and child (and even the very young) in an atmosphere of holiness and devoutness; to gather them for the purpose which was the very essence of the Mitzva of 'Hakhel' as stated in the Torah: "In order that they should listen and that they should learn, and should fear G-d, your G-d, and observe all the words of this Torah".[2]

It is particularly the duty of everyone who is a 'king', a leader in his environment—the spiritual leader in his congregation, the teacher in his classroom, the father in his family—to raise the voice of Torah and Mitzvos, forcefully and earnestly, so that it create a profound impression and an abiding influence in his sphere, an influence that should be translated in daily life into conduct governed by the Torah and Mitzvos, with fear of heaven and, at the same time, gladness of heart.

REFERENCES:
    Based on an excerpt of a talk by the Lubavitcher Rebbe א״טליט   published in the "Lubavitch News Service" publication.
    1) Deuteronomy 31:12
    2) Ibid.

AHAVAS YISROEL

On Simchas Torah Jews of all ages throughout the world crowd the synagogues singing and dancing joyously, carrying the Torah scrolls on their shoulders. During this happy festival, three great loves become revealed—"Ahavas Hashem" (Love of G-d), "Ahavas HaTorah" (Love of the Torah) and "Ahavas Yisroel" (Love of our fellow Jews). Let us examine some Chassidic teachings about "Ahavas Yisroel", the Mitzva which commands us to love another from the depths of the heart.

* * *

The founders and early leaders of Chassidism often spoke about Ahavas Yisroel; the great 'Maggid' (preacher) of Mezritch, successor to the Baal Shem Tov, was served by his pupils in 'shifts'. During the 'shift' of Rabbi Elimelech of Lizensk, the Maggid once called to him, "Meilech! Hear what they say in the Yeshivah of Heaven. They say that Ahavas Yisroel means to love the completely wicked just as you love a 'tsaddik'—the completely righteous!"[1]

The Maggid's pupil, the Alter Rebbe, founder of Chabad Chassidism, described Ahavas Yisroel as a love that extends to every Jew "great or small", the love binding brothers, inbred, instinctive, "essential love,[2]" unrelated to, and unaffected by, appearance, personality or conduct.

"Love your fellow as yourself"[3], means that the love of another must be the same as one's self-love. Love for one's self is not based on his virtues. One does not think, "I am talented, wise, good, and righteous and I deserve to be loved, therefore, I shall love myself". Love of self is not predicated on quality of character, it is part of his personality and will conceal even the worst traits. As King Solomon said, "(self)—Love covers all transgressions."[4] This does not mean that a person's self-love makes him ignorant of his faults. He recognizes them but is unaffected by them—and this is precisely the kind of love that the Torah commands us to show towards our fellows.

REFERENCES:
Based on Likuttei Sichos Vol. II pp. 299-301.
1) See Tomar Devorah Cap. 2.
2) See Tanya Cap. 32.
3) Leviticus 19:18.
4) Proverbs 10:12.

SUPPLEMENT
GEMS OF CHASSIDIC WISDOM

"A STONE WILL SHOUT . . ."

Concerning the Messianic future, it is written: "A stone will shout from the wall, the branches of the trees will answer them." *Now* the inanimate creatures are quiet. One steps on a stone and it is silent, but there will be a time of revelations in the future when inanimate objects will speak. They will demand of man and ask him whether he thought or spoke the words of Torah, while walking on them with his feet. The earth has suffered in silence and in patience for thousands of years, from the very first beginning of creation and many creatures have stepped on it. It has borne all this with the hope that some day a Jew will walk on it, meet another, and the two will converse of Torah. If they do not speak a word of Torah while walking through the street, the earth will say to them: "You are also like an animal."

Hayom Yom, Adar I, 15

"AIR POLLUTION"

Human life depends on the air we breathe. Without air one cannot live. The atmosphere in which we live and breathe shapes our lives. One who lives in an air of Torah and Mitzvoth lives a healthy life. He who lives in an air of denial (of G-d's reality) and cynicism lives a diseased life. He is ever in danger of being further infected by contagion. The very first general step of therapy is to purify the air. The work of purifying the air is the obligation of those who know Torah and are well read in the holy books. Air is purified by a process of passing it through a filter made up of letters of Torah. Standing in one's store, walking in the street or traveling in the subway, one can clean the air by reciting passages of Torah. Everyone who knows how to read holy books, how to study Torah, needs to learn some Chumash, the Psalms, the Mishnah, Tanya by heart. No matter where or when, he will be able to think, meditate and recite the holy letters of the Torah.

Hayom Yom, Teves 11

LENGTH OF DAYS

When the Alter Rebbe wanted to bless Reb Yekusiel of Lyeplia with riches, the latter said that he doesn't desire them for they would only distract him from the study of Chassiduth and his work of serving G-d. And when the Rebbe wanted to bless him with length of days, he said: "But not with a peasant's years, years in which one has eyes and doesn't see, ears and doesn't hear, in which one doesn't see the Divine and doesn't hear the Divine."

Hayom Yom, Cheshvan 6

ISRAEL . . . AND THE STARS

Israel has been compared to the stars, which shine in the highest Heavens. He who relies on their guidance, will not err even in the darkest night.

Each single Jew, man or woman, has the moral strength and spiritual power to influence his surrounding, his acquaintances, with the light of Torah.

Hayom Yom, Cheshvan 5

SOLDIERS AND SERVANTS

From the day on which the Children of Israel left Egypt, they were called the "armies of the L-rd." There is a fundamental difference between a "servant" and a "soldier." The Children of Israel were also called servants. A servant does the work of his master. There are all sorts of levels in the work a master assigns to him. He tells him to pierce pearls or to do other kinds of work, or charges him with simpler tasks. Though a great deal of effort, great bother and trouble are necessary in obedience, it still does not call for one to lay down his life. But soldiers are servants who serve with great effort and trouble and are called up to offer their lives. They do this in both protective and offensive wars. For, it is their task to stand on guard with the greatest strength, without ever becoming frightened of the enemy and the opponent. The work of the soldier is not in mental attainment. His task is to follow orders. And, so it was with the souls of Israel in Egypt who, due to their great affliction and bitter pain were at their lowest level. And, nevertheless, they did not change their names, language or clothes and remained on guard with the greatest strength. They knew that the Holy One, blessed be He, had promised to redeem them. He, who comports himself in such a manner, belongs to the armies of the L-rd. The L-rd helps his "soldiers" in ways transcending those of nature.

Hayom Yom, Nissan 12

THE INDIVIDUAL JEW:

It is said, "The whole sun is reflected in a drop of water." In the same way is the whole of our nation reflected in each individual, and what is true of the nation as a whole is true of the individual.

EFFORT:

The road is not free from obstacles and obstructions, for in the Divine order of things we are expected to attain our goal by *effort*. Once we make a determined effort, though, success is Divinely assured, and the obstacles which at first loomed large, dissolve and disappear.

FAITH, NOT FEAR:

The core of Jewish vitality and indestructibility is pure faith in G-d; not in an abstract Deity, hidden somewhere in the heavenly spheres, who watches this world from a distance; but in a very personal G-d, who is the life and existence of everybody and who permeates where one is and what one does. Where there is such faith there is no room for fear or anxiety, as the Psalmist says, "I fear no evil, for You are with me"; with me *at all times,* not only on Shabbos and Yomtov, or during prayer and meditation on G-d.

JOY VERSUS DEPRESSION:

Even in the case of spiritual failure, no Jew should feel depressed; a feeling of depression and gloom is, in itself, one of the strategic weapons which the Yetzer Hora (Evil Inclination) uses, in an effort to discourage a person from serving G-d with joy and alacrity. And, when the Yetzer Horah succeeds in one thing, he does for further things.

The way to combat the Yetzer Horah is to call forth redoubled efforts on one's part to overcome the feeling of depression, and replace it with a feeling of joy in the realization that no matter what the past has been, it is always possible to attach oneself to G-d, through the study of the Torah, and the observance of the Mitzvos.

Thus, in the final analysis, it is up to a person to overcome his difficulties by his own effort and determination, and we have already been assured that where there is a determined effort, success is certain.

"MOUNTAIN CLIMBING":

". . . I was especially pleased to read that you realize that there is a great deal more to do. For the realization that there is more to be done ought to bring forth additional forces to meet the challenge. All the more so, since every one of us is commanded to go from strength to strength in all matters of holiness. In this connection it is well to remember the saying of my father-in-law, of saintly memory, that in these times every Jew should consider himself a mountain-climber scaling a steep mountain. In this situation he must either continue to climb — or slide back, for he cannot remain stationary. It is also a well-known law of physics that the rate of a falling object accelerates. . . . The lesson is obvious."

FAITH AND INTELLECT:

The wisest of all men, King Solomon, said: "G-d made man straight, but they sought many accounts." Man often confuses himself with delving, unnecessarily, into inquiries and accounts of matters of religion which should be taken for granted and which do not really present any problems. In fact, the more intellectual a person is, the more he is inclined to seek "accounts" and, consequently, the more apt he is to get confused.

This brings to mind an amusing incident that involved a professor of medicine. He was once learning anatomy — particularly the anatomy of the leg, describing the hundreds of muscles which are so perfectly coordinated in the motion of the leg during walking. He became so engrossed in the details (all the more so being a man of great intellect) that momentarily he found his walking difficult and quite complicated as he began to analyze the working of each muscle and joint!

THE SHOFAR:

Rosh Hashanah is the anniversary of the creation of Man, the last of all creatures and the highest in the order of development. Man's preeminence over beast is in his intellect.

One would have thought, therefore, that the Rosh Hashanah service would be highlighted by intellectual dissertations and discussions, in which Man could demonstrate his superiority over all other forms of creation.

Yet, the highlight of the Rosh Hashanah service is *Tekias-Shofar,* a simple ceremony of sounding a ram's horn. Even in ancient days there existed fine musical instruments, as is historically known. But the delicate and refined strains of music of all musical instruments will not do. The commandment of Tekias-Shofar specifically requires the use of a simple horn, producing simple sounds.

There is a profound lesson in this: Rosh Hashanah, the beginning and foundation of the whole year, is inaugurated through the sounding of the horn of a beast to teach us that although Man is an intellectual creature and must use his intellect in his daily life, the basis of his intellectual life must be submission to G-d, with the absolute submissiveness of the intellect-lacking beast.

Art.

. . . I would like to take this opportunity to make a further point, which I had occasion to mention to our very distinguished friend Mr.

Chaim Yaakov Lipchitz who, I am glad to note, is going to open the Exhibition. I have known Mr. Lipchitz for many years, and know of his sincere interest in all good things, especially those connected with our people. The point is that those who have been Divinely gifted in art, whether sculpture or painting and the like, have the privilege of being able to convert an inanimate thing, such as a brush, paint and canvass, or wood and stone, etc., into living form. In a deeper sense it is the ability to transform to a certain extent the material into spiritual, even where the creation is in still life, and certainly where the artistic work has to do with living creatures and humans. How much more so if the art medium is used to advance ideas, especially reflecting Torah and Mitzvoth, which would raise the artistic skill to its highest level.

Indeed, this is the ultimate purpose of the Exhibition, which hopefully will impress and inspire the viewers with higher emotions and concepts of Yiddishkeit imbued with the spirit of Chassidus, and make them, too, vehicles of disseminating Yiddishkeit in their environment, and particularly through the educational institutions.

FOOD FOR THE SOUL

The Mitzvos which a Jew performs in his daily life are not 'symbolic' but are good deeds in themselves, first of all for his own well-being and also for his entire environment. If the pragmatic value of such Mitzvos is not fully, or even partially, grasped readily, that does not alter the case, as may be explained by way of a simile: when the body is in need of food, it must be fed without a preliminary study as to how the vitamins and calories sustain it; likewise in the case of the soul, whose 'food' and sustenance are the Torah and Mitzvos. When the soul is hungry, *especially when it is so starved that it does not even feel any appetite*, the first thing is to sustain it by Torah and practical Mitzvos-observance.

Indeed, it should not be surprising that the profundity of G-d's precepts is not readily grasp-able. Compare the attitude of a child towards the injunctions of a great professor giving him a code of conduct: considering the vast difference in the intellects of the two, it would not be sur-prising if the child cannot understand the pro-fessor, although the difference in knowledge and experience is here only relative, and the child has the potentialities to attain the professor's standing in due course, and perhaps even exceed him. This is not the case in the relationship of a human being to G-d, even if that human being is a prophet. No man can grasp the Divine wis-dom, except in so far as G-d in His kindness has enabled us to do so when we follow His com-mands and precepts and live accordingly.

NUMBER TEN

The figure "Ten" concludes the order of the *single numbers,* and begins the order of the *ten's.* It marks a transition to a higher plane—not ony *quantitatively* but also *qualitatively.* From the figure ten and up begins a new order, which is not only higher in number, but is also of an infinitely higher category.

This is one of the explanations why the figure ten has a special significance in the Torah; hence also in Jewish life. This significance expresses itself in the law which requires a quorum of ten Jews (a "Minyan") in the performance of sacred occasions and certain prayers (such as Borchu, Kaddish, Kedusho and the like). This law is derived from a verse in this week's portion, namely, *I shall be sanctified in the midst of the children of Israel* (22:32). For although each Jew, as an individual, is precious and holy, it is quite different when ten Jews get together, thereby creating a *Tzibbur* (congregation) which assumes a very high order of holiness, wherein the individual, too, is elevated to a much higher level of holiness.

Rabbi Sholom Dov Ber of Lubavitch of saintly memory, was once asked, "What is a Chosid?" and he replied, "A Chosid is a 'street-lamp lighter.' " (In olden days there used to be a man whose job was to light the street-lamps by means of a light which he carried at the end of a long pole). The lamps were there in readiness, but they needed to be lit. Sometimes the lamps are not as easily accessible as lamps on street corners; there are lamps in forsaken places, or at sea, but there must be someone to light even those lamps, so that they should not be wasted, but should light up the path of others.

It is written, "the soul of man is the lamp of G-d." It is also written, "A Mitzvah is a candle, and the Torah is the light."

A Chosid is one who puts his personal affairs aside and goes around lighting up the souls of Jews with the light of the Torah and Mitzvoth. Jewish souls are in readiness to be lit; sometimes they are around the corner, sometimes they are in a desert or at sea. There must be someone who, disregarding his own comforts and conveniences, will go out to put a light to those "lamps." This is the function of a true Chosid.

* * *

The message is obvious. It only remains to be added that this function is not really limited to Chasidim, but it is the function of every Jew.

"BY THE SWEAT OF THY BROW . . ."

Rabbi Shneur Zalman of Liadi, known as the 'Alter Rebbe', founder of Chabad Chassidism, was one of the most illustrious scholars and Talmudists of his time. He was also the 'Rebbe' (leader) of thousands of Chassidim and his fame as a Tzaddik (righteous and holy man) had spread far and wide. It was common knowledge that when Alter Rebbe gave someone his Brocho (blessing) for success in any particular endeavor, that fortunate individual would succeed greatly in his venture. The Alter Rebbe's grandson, Menachem Mendel, having been orphaned at an early age, was brought up in his grandfather's house. Consequently, he was more keenly aware of his grandfather's greatness and holiness than many of the Alter Rebbe's followers and he was better able to appreciate the great value of his grandfather's Brocho.

On one occasion the Alter Rebbe wished to give his brilliant grandson a Brocho for success in Torah study. The boy, much to everyone's surprise, declined the offer! He maintained that Torah scholarship *must* be acquired through *labor*. He wanted his success in Torah-study to be the result of his *own* toil.

Years later he expressed regret at his earlier recision. Said he: "I could have accepted the brocho and with its help I would have reached a certain level of Torah scholarship. I could *then* have utilized my own efforts to succeed in Torah-study above and beyond that level!"

Menachem Mendel grew up to become the famed "Tsemach Tsedek", third successor to the leadership of Chabad Chassidism and a Rabbi and Torah-scholar of prodigious genius.

CONTRADICTORY CONDUCT?

(The following two anecdotes are based on the words of our sages, "Love all people and draw them close to Torah. One interpretation of these words is that although one must show love to all people, one must be careful to draw them close to Torah and not the Torah to them.)

"LOVE *ALL* PEOPLE . . .

The previous Lubavitcher Rebbe of sainted memory required of his followers that they occupy themselves with be-friending even simple, unlettered, and often unobservant Jews. What is more, he expected his Chassidim to teach and instruct these individuals even in such simple matters as "Alef-Beis"; either "Alef-Beis" in the plain sense of the term or - the 'Alef-Beis' (i. e. first steps) of returning to G-d and observing the Mitzvos.

". . . . DRAW *THEM* CLOSE TO TORAH (NOT THE *TORAH* TO THEM)

At a certain Rabbinical conference, at which various solutions to the problem of the assimilation of contemporary Jews were discussed, a delegate defended the policy of partial compromise, bringing the Torah 'down to the level of the people'. He said: "today a fire is burning in the Jewish community — the fire of assimilation. Now, although drinking-water must indeed be pure, surely *anything* is good enough to extinguish a *fire*—even dirty and impure water."

The previous Lubvitcher Rebbe of sainted memory, who was present at the meeting retorted: "That is true if the liquid is definitely *water* and the only question is whether it is clean water or impure water. If, however, one should seize a bucket of liquid and throw it into a raging fire in an attempt to quench the flames, and if that liquid should prove to be, not water at all, but kerosene . . . ! What then?"

ICE . . . AND IDOLATRY

The saintly Baal Shem Tov, founder of Chassidism, taught his followers that whatever one sees or hears, whatever occurrence one chances to witness, has some connection and relationship to himself. For, since nothing in this world transpires without the guiding hand of Hashgocho Protis (Divine Providence), it is evident that this particular happening is relevant to *him* and the Almighty desired him to observe it so that he might derive therefrom some lesson and instruction.

One wintry day the Baal Shem Tov and some of his disciples passed by a frozen river. A group of peasants, members of a pagan idolatrous sect, were busily engaged in carving an idol out of the ice, to use for one of their heathen ceremonies. The Baal Shem's pupils became depressed. Pondering on their master's explanation of 'Hashgocho Protis' they thought to themselves: "What possible connection could *we* have with pagan idolatry!? Why were we guided by Divine Providence to witness this scene? What lesson or instruction are we expected to derive from it?"

They turned to their great Rebbe for guidance. Said the Baal Shem Tov: "Water, as we see in the Torah, cleanses spiritual impurities. Anyone who became defiled and unclean would immerse in *water* to become clean again; the basis of family purity - Taharas Hamishpacha - is that the women immerse in the *waters* of the Mikvah (Ritualarium); on rising, the Jew washes his hands to rid them of the spiritual impurities of the night, and so on."

"In short, water is the very source of spiritual purity and holiness. But, when it becomes *cold* and frozen . . . it can even become an *idol!*"

*   •   •   •

Yes, it is but a short step from icy indifference (to Yiddishkeit) to complete cynicism.

THE WHEEL OF FORTUNE

Rabbi Sholom Ber of Lubavitch once said: "The fortunes of man in the world are like a turning wheel.

There are two kinds of fool. He who sits atop the wheel and laughs - is a fool. 'Idiot', we may call to him, 'what are you laughing at? Admittedly you are "on top of the world" at this moment, but it is nothing more than a revolving wheel. Should the wheel turn, you may find yourself lower than those at whom you previously laughed!

He who lies beneath the wheel and bewails his fate—is also a fool. 'Simpleton', we may say to him, 'why do you cry? Do you not realize that your fortunes are merely a turning wheel?! Indeed, the very fact that you are now at the *lowest* point of the wheel's rotation, means that with the wheel's *very next* movement you will be elevated; your fortunes will improve.'

*   *   *   *

He who is wealthy and fortunate and sits "atop the wheel" should contemplate that his material fortune is, after all, nothing more than a constantly revolving wheel; it has no enduring worth. But a verse of Chumash (Torah), a verse of T'hillim (psalms), or a good turn to one's fellow-Jew, *these* endure for ever".